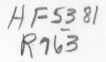

Occupations and Values

by MORRIS ROSENBERG

With the Assistance of
EDWARD A. SUCHMAN and ROSE K. GOLDSEN

The Free Press, Glencoe, Illinois

PREFACE

The present study of occupational choice grew out of an initial interest in the subject of social values. Sociological and anthropological theory and research had made it increasingly evident that the understanding of human behavior required a sound knowledge of the system of values characteristic of various cultures. As a consequence, in 1949 a number of social scientists and philosophers at Cornell University participated in a faculty seminar designed to pool and develop thought and knowledge on the subject of values.

The following year, with the support of a generous grant from the Carnegie Corporation of New York, an empirical study of college students' values was launched at Cornell. A representative sample of 2,758 students were queried about their occupational, educational, economic, political, religious, and social values. In 1952 a new values study, placing special stress on students' reactions to the prospect of impending military service but also including data on occupational and other values, was conducted with 4,585 college students selected on a representative basis from eleven universities throughout the country. In the second study, it proved possible to re-interview 944 Cornellians who had participated in the first investigation, thus enabling us to examine trends and changes in the values, attitudes, and behavior of these people.

A key area of interest in these studies was the problem of occupational choices and occupational values; as a consequence, a large number of items were included in both studies which were designed to shed light on the determinants of occupational choices and on the special role which values played in directing the occupational decision. The present report is based upon the analysis of these data.

There are many people to whom grateful acknowledgment is due for their kind cooperation and help in the collection and analysis of the data. We are grateful to those faculty members of other universities who aided us by their careful selection of student samples at their institutions and their administration of the questionnaires. The nation-wide survey would not have been possible without the aid of Albert H. Hastorf, Dartmouth College; Donald N. Elliott,

Wayne University; Preston Valien, Fisk University; William
S. Robinson and S. F. Camilleri, University of California at
Los Angeles; Daniel O. Price, University of North Carolina;
David C. McClelland and Martha Williamson, Wesleyan University;
Peter H. Rossi, Harvard University; Fred L. Strodtbeck, Yale
University; Dwight Chapman and Walter Crockett, University
of Michigan; and Wayne Holtzman, University of Texas.

A number of people have been very generous in their expend-
itures of time and effort on this study. Robert K. Merton
has carefully examined various drafts of the manuscript and
has offered many sound, imaginative, and thought-provoking
suggestions. His help and encouragement have been most helpful in making the present volume a reality. My friend and
teacher, Paul F. Lazarsfeld, has kindly given me the benefit
of his advice in various parts of the study; in particular,
I owe a debt to him for his help in the analysis of behavioral
and attitudinal change. Patricia L. Kendall was kind enough
to offer many insightful criticisms of an earlier draft of
the present report. Finally, Robin M. Williams, Jr., has
been a participant in this study from its inception. The entire study, from the formulation of the questionnaire to the
analysis of the data, has benefited enormously from his important contributions to the understanding of the nature of
values. Drs. Merton, Lazarsfeld, Kendall, and Williams are,
of course, in no way responsible for the defects of the present study.

The present investigation was supported by generous grants
from the Carnegie Corporation of New York. Some of the data
to be presented were analyzed while the senior author was a
Research Training Fellow of the Social Science Research
Council. We wish to acknowledge our gratitude to these organizations for their help and encouragement. It should be un-
derstood, however, that they are not responsible for anything
which appears on the following pages.

Morris Rosenberg
Stanford, California
January, 1957

CONTENTS

CHAPTER I

INTRODUCTION

Throughout our lives we are constantly making decisions—whether to listen to one radio program or another, whether to vote for one candidate or another, whether to take a long, short, or no vacation, whether to buy a Ford, Plymouth, Chevrolet, Buick, etc. Whether it is a matter of deciding what to have for breakfast or deciding what college to enroll in, the common characteristic is that we must make a choice from among a certain range of alternatives.

When you get right down to it, however, there aren't many really "big" decisions that we have to make in our lifetimes—decisions which involve very long-term commitments, which influence our chances for living full, rich, satisfying lives, which influence our thoughts, feelings, and actions for years to come. One of these "big" decisions is marriage—whether to marry and, if so, to whom. Another is choosing one's life work—whether to work at this job or that. Neither of the choices is completely irrevocable—we can change mates or change professions—but there is a widespread tendency in American middle-class society to view them as *final* decisions, and they are as important a pair of long-term commitments as we are ever likely to make. Although we may stew and fret over things, most other decisions are either relatively trivial (should we drive to work or take the bus) or subsidiary to these major decisions (having selected law as a profession, which law school should we choose).

It is plain that the selection of a particular kind of work has important implications both for the individual and for the total society. Every society must somehow arrange to get people to do what has to get done in order to enable the society to keep going and prosper. It must so distribute its human resources, both in quantity and quality, that societal needs will be satisfied.

Two recent sources of concern highlight this point. The first is a report that Russia is currently producing a larger

quantity of adequately trained engineers and scientists than
the United States;[1] the second is the existence of teacher
shortages in various parts of the country.[2] Thus, if young
John Smith decides to become a lawyer rather than an engineer
"because I can make more money that way," this decision has
implications for the global economic and power position of
the United States five or ten years hence. Or if a girl decides to become an actress rather than a teacher, the quality
of education given to school children in the future will be
affected. There is no assurance that the sometimes arbitrary
and whimsical occupational decisions of contemporary American
youth will gear into the concrete needs of the society of the
future. In many cases it is certain that they will not; in
these cases, society is faced with a maldistribution of its
human resources, and must necessarily function below the
level of maximum efficiency.

From the viewpoint of the individual, work will importantly influence diverse aspects of his life. The individual's
status in the community, based on the esteem in which his
fellows hold him, will largely depend on the work he does and
how well he does it. These evaluations by others will be reflected in the mirror of his mind to influence the individual's evaluation of himself; thus his self-esteem or self-
confidence will to some extent hinge upon his occupational
choice and performance. Furthermore, every individual has
certain creative potentialities which find greater or lesser
expression in work. Part of the richness of human experience
lies in our ability to spend ourselves in an activity which
challenges and draws out our highest potentialities. Consequently, the chances of living a life characterized by productiveness, self-actualization, and self-fulfillment will
depend to an important extent on the degree to which our work
allows us to exercise our creative potentialities.

Then there is the question of rewards—especially money
and power. The enjoyment of material goods and services, and
the opportunity to follow a characteristic style of life
hinges largely on the remuneration one receives from work.
The individual choosing an occupation, therefore, must do so
with reference to a whole host of subsidiary wants which the
extrinsic rewards of work can potentially satisfy.

Another way in which an individual's work will tend to
affect his life is in the requirement to play a certain occupational role. To some extent the doctor or teacher must behave in a way which the society has defined as appropriate
for one occupying such a status. Thus the individual who
makes an occupational choice also commits himself to a certain

pattern of thought and behavior for years to come. In many
cases, if the role is sufficiently internalized, it may influence his entire personality structure. In addition, the
individual's interaction with other human beings, which
tends to be the source of most gratifications, is influenced
by the nature of his occupation.

It is obvious, then, that the individual's occupational
decision has important implications both for society and for
his future life activity and satisfactions. And yet he must
usually make this decision on the basis of a very vague and
tenuous knowledge of the relevant facts. In the first place,
the individual tends to be unclear about his own talents,
since many of these can only find expression in actual occupational practice. Secondly, he can only make a more or
less well-founded guess concerning the sorts of skills and
talents which will be needed in the society of the future.
Finally, his picture of the requirements and rewards of an
occupation is seldom based on the foundation of actual experience; more often it represents a series of haphazard im-
pressions gained from diverse sources. Thus, faced with a
vast variety of occupations from which to choose, and pos-
sessing an inadequate knowledge of himself, future social
needs, and occupational requirements and rewards, the individual is *compelled* to make his own single decision which,
he realizes, is life-long in its implications. He is like
a hungry child with a coin looking at a long counter of
sweets which he has never tasted who must decide on one purchase—and who doesn't know the value of his money. The
pattern of free occupational choice characteristic of
American society is calculated to enable people to realize
their highest potentialities, but it may also spin a complex
web of psychological conflict.

The present study is an investigation of this process of
occupational choice among college students. There are several reasons why it is important to study the way these
people make up their minds.

The college youth of today are the occupational elite of
tomorrow. On their present decisions hinge the fate of industry, commerce, politics, the professions, the arts and
sciences, the educational system of the future. This, then,
is a particularly crucial group to study—the people who
will occupy the key social positions in time to come.

Not only are college students an important group to
study, but the *time* at which we study them—during their
college years—is a period of central significance in the
occupational decision process. For these are the years in

which the individual tends to make up his mind, to reach the
point of final decision. At college, the student's ideas
about work are still relatively undistorted by the special
conditions of the job situation in which he will eventually
find himself; it is therefore easier to observe the influence of certain abstract factors, such as values, attitudes,
personality structure, and images, as they bear on the decision process. To observe the student while he is in college
also makes it possible to study change and development of
occupational choice, the flow in and out of various occupations, the mutual interaction of occupational choices and
values, and the resolution of occupational conflicts.

Furthermore, the decision reached at college is likely to
have a long-lasting effect. Take the case of a student who
chooses a profession. Such fields tend to require so much
specialized training that the student making this choice
makes a more serious and long-term commitment than, let us
say, a manual worker. Whereas the semiskilled worker may
shift around from job to job or industry to industry, the
man who studies medicine is likely to practice this occupation for the remainder of his life. Thus, the economic,
social, and psychological implications of the college student's choice are of particular seriousness and importance.

In American society, the student making an occupational
decision has about 40,000 occupations from which to choose.[3]
Were he to give serious consideration to all 40,000 of them,
he would probably have little hope of keeping his sanity.
How, then, does he finally settle on a specific choice?

It is possible to visualize the occupational decision
process as a series of *progressive delimitations of alternatives*. A number of factors in the individual and in society
operate to cut down the broad range of occupational possibilities available. The bases for the elimination vary:
some occupations are not *socially appropriate* for an individual occupying a certain social status; some occupations
are not *possible* for an individual with certain characteristics, knowledge, and resources; and some occupations are not
desirable for an individual with certain values, attitudes,
and personality characteristics.

The range of occupational alternatives is delimited,
first of all, by the student's statuses and roles. Most
college students stem from middle- and upper-class families.
In terms of the values, orientations, and life-styles of
these people, thousands of manual and lower-level white-
collar occupations are *immediately and automatically eliminated from serious consideration*. The effective alterna-

tives, then, are restricted to higher-level business activities and to the professions. It is within this very limited range that a choice is made.

A further broad delimitation is imposed by the individual's sex status. Some fields (e. g., engineering, medicine) tend to be considered appropriate only for men; others, such as primary school teaching, are considered "women's fields." Thus, men and women immediately eliminate hundreds of fields which are socially accepted as the province of the other sex.

Racial, religious, and nationality factors also enter into the progressive delimitation of occupational alternatives. The fact of occupational and educational discrimination often makes it so difficult, if not impossible, for the minority group member to gain admittance to certain occupations and to pursue them successfully that he may eliminate them from consideration entirely.

The range of occupational alternatives is further narrowed by what one might call the "social publicity" of the occupation. A recent study, for example, showed that 97% of the population could not give a satisfactorily exact definition or explanation of what a "nuclear physicist" was.[4] There are probably hundreds, or even thousands, of occupations with which most people either have slight or no acquaintance: plant pathologist, biostatistician, paleontologist, ichthyologist, entomologist, and so on. Occupations which are outside the individual's purview obviously are eliminated as candidates for consideration.

In addition, there is the intrusion into the decision process of a broad system of "reality factors" centering, on the one hand, about the individual's physical endowments, mental capacities, and material resources and, on the other, about the availability of jobs. A man with a weak, puny body can hardly become a professional wrestler; a man with a weak, puny intellect can hardly become a professional chess player or mathematician; and a man with a weak, puny bank balance can hardly become a great financier. There are exceptions, of course, but there are many people who will eliminate from consideration those occupations which require extraordinary talents or resources. With regard to the factor of availability of jobs, finally, a boy may be an excellent softball player but may abandon hope of making a career out of it when he learns of the limitations of professional opportunities in the field.

There are, of course, many people who resist the influence of the general channeling factors we have mentioned— middle-class children becoming auto mechanics, women becoming

doctors and lawyers, poor boys becoming captains of industry.
Furthermore, many people may not perform these automatic
eliminations, accepting certain occupations as real alternatives, despite their awareness of the special problems involved; in this case, these alternatives do enter into the
occupational decision process. For most people, however,
the overwhelming bulk of occupational alternatives are immediately eliminated from, or never enter into, serious consideration. By the time the student reaches college, there
are only a *relatively* small number of occupations which remain candidates for selection. Generally speaking, the individual's decision is limited to those occupations about
which he knows something, which are appropriate to his class
position and sex status, which are not barred by ethnic discrimination or by limitations of physical and mental endowments and material resources, and in which realistic opportunities for occupational practice exist.

Yet all this still does not enable the individual to settle on a single occupation. How does he choose from among
the many fields which continue to remain open to him? In
order to answer this question, it is necessary to consider
some of the basic internal characteristics of the individual—his values, attitudes, and personality needs—in order
to see how they bear on the occupational decision process.

Values—Whenever an individual makes a selection from a
given number of alternatives, it is likely that some *value*
is behind the decision. An occupational choice is not a
value, but it is made on the basis of values. For a value
is "a conception...of the desirable... ";[5] "values are...
'things' in which people are interested—things they want,
desire to be or become, feel as obligatory, worship, enjoy."[6]
When an individual chooses an occupation, he thinks there is
something "good" about it, and this conception of the "good"
is part of an internalized mental structure which establishes priorities regarding what he wants out of life. To
ask what an individual wants out of his work is to a large
extent to ask what he wants out of his life. It is therefore indispensable to an adequate understanding of the occupational decision process to consider what people want or
consider good or desirable, for these are the essential criteria by which choices are made.

Attitudes—Occupational choices are also influenced by
certain overarching *attitudes* which condition the individual's perception of diverse aspects of the world. One such
attitude would be faith in people—whether one feels that

human beings are basically selfish and untrustworthy or generous and kind. The importance of studying the individual's
degree of faith in people lies in the fact that occupational
activity is to a large extent a system of interpersonal relationships; consequently, the way one feels about people
will influence one's feelings about various kinds of work.
Basic attitudes of this sort, which importantly influence
one's orientation toward many aspects of social life, are
obviously relevant to occupational choice.

Personality needs—Another factor which enters into the
progressive delimitation of occupational alternatives is the
degree of harmony between the behavioral requirements of the
occupation and the *personality structure* of the individual.
A shy, timid, retiring individual is unlikely to aspire to
become an army top sergeant in charge of an infantry platoon.
An insecure person with a compulsive need for predictability
might be expected to eschew the occupation of free-lance
photographer. The purpose of citing such extreme examples
is to make it clear that personality factors cannot be ig-
nored in considering occupational choice.

Our viewpoint, then, is that the occupational decision
process may be visualized as a series of progressive delimitations of alternatives. In the following three chapters
we will consider the influence of the internal factors on
occupational choice—values, attitudes, and personality
characteristics. In Chapter V we turn to a consideration of
the influence of status and role factors on occupational
choices and values.

The complexity of the decision process is highlighted by
the observation that not only may values influence occupational choices, but choices may influence values as well.
This is likely to occur when an individual who has made an
occupational choice begins to internalize the values, attitudes, and behavioral patterns characteristic of actual occupational incumbents—a process which Robert K. Merton has
termed "anticipatory socialization." Throughout this
study, then, we will be concerned with the interrelation-
ships among the factors which enter into the occupational
decision process.

Change of occupational choice—At several points we have
referred to occupational choice as a *process*. To conceive
of choice in these terms is to accentuate the notion that
movement, development, change are involved in reaching a
decision. People who make up their minds can also change
their minds; and the problem is to understand if, how, and
why college students shift their occupational preferences

during the course of their college careers. How stable is an
occupational decision? Does the passage of time and the in-
crement of new experience lead to a flow out of certain occupations and into certain others? What happens to the people
in conflict—people whose occupational choices and values are
"inconsistent," who violate the occupational norms characteristic of their sexes, who choose occupations beyond their
capacities, whose ideology is opposed to the requirements of
their occupations? Does greater change occur in some occupations than in others? Are there some people who are disposed
to change irrespective of the area of decision involved?
Questions of this sort, which are examined in Chapters VI and
VII, are designed to move us in the direction of the *dynamic*
analysis of social research data, and some recent technical
developments in the analysis of panel data have facilitated
this approach.

   Conflict—In any decision process, the possibility of conflict exists; the individual must make a choice from a given
range of alternatives. Other things equal, the fewer the alternatives, the less evenly weighted their advantages, and
the less important the decision, the less is emotional stress
likely to be generated. In the occupational decision process, there are many alternatives which may be considered at
various times. Since every occupation has certain advantages
and disadvantages, inducements and shortcomings, it is rare
that the balance should be overwhelmingly weighted in favor
of a single occupation *vis-a-vis* all other alternatives.

   The likelihood of conflict is enhanced by the multiplicity
of elements which enter into the decision process. In principle, the individual may weigh occupation against occupation, value against value, personality against value, value
against reality, ends against means, and so on. Such problems need not necessarily erupt into conflicts, of course,
but in many cases they do. Throughout this study, then, we
will be constantly concerned with the theme of conflict and
the problem of conflict resolution.

   There are two special types of conflict, however, to
which we have devoted special attention. The first is the
conflict between ends and means. Both the ends of occupational action and the means of achieving them are usually
based on a system of internalized societal values. Problems
arise, however, when certain means, which are acceptable to
the individual's system of values, prove ineffective in enabling him to attain his ends, or when other means, which are
effective in attaining the desired ends, conflict with his
values. Assume, for example, that a young man has chosen a

particular occupation because he wants to make a good deal
of money, but realizes that, in order to do so, he must use
means which affront society's moral sensibilities. What
does he do? Does he abandon the goal, maintain the goal but
abandon his scruples about the means, or keep them both and
try to live with his conflict? These problems will be considered in Chapter VIII.

The other conflict is that between occupational aspirations and occupational expectations. Many students would
like to enter one occupation but actually expect to enter
another. Here we have a potentially serious source of frustration—the occupations to which students aspire are for
various reasons beyond their reach. How such conflicts came
about, who faces them, and how they are finally resolved,
are the questions considered in Chapter IX.

These, then, represent our central themes—decision making, decision change, decision conflict. It is hoped that
the empirical data to be presented will shed light on the
social psychology of the decision process at the same time
that it provides material of relevance to the sociology of
occupations.

CRITERIA FOR CAREER CHOICE

Occupational Values

The college student who makes an occupational choice is
projecting his vision into the long future. He knows that
the freshest and most alert hours of his waking life will be
spent at his work. Therefore, to ask what he wants out of
his work to an important extent is to ask what he wants out
of his life.

Work has meant many things to men throughout history; it
has served as an "expiation of sin," as a path to salvation,
as a means of self-actualization.[1] Today, Mills maintains,
the chief meaning of work for the modern white-collar person
lies in income, status, and power.[2] Similarly, Gurko has
commented on the "cash-register" orientation of many modern
Americans:

> College students wondering whether to major in his-
> tory or English literature are often dissuaded by the
> question: What can you do with it when you get out?
> Does anyone want to write? It makes sense only if he
> aims at the jackpot. Would he enjoy teaching? There's
> more money in advertising. Careers, and indeed life
> experiences, are selected not on the basis of their
> personal satisfactions or social usefulness, but
> strictly in cash-register terms.[3]

Actually, this "what's in it for me" attitude does not
appear to be nearly so prevalent as some observers would
have us believe. For example, the members of our nationwide
cross-section of college students were presented with a list
of occupational values and were told to "consider to what
extent a job or career would have to satisfy each of these
requirements before you could consider it IDEAL." They
were instructed to rank these values as high, medium, or

low in importance, and then to indicate the relative importance of those values marked high.

It turns out that students view work as more than simply
a means of making money; indeed, the range of values which
they hope to satisfy in their occupations is very wide. As
Table 1 shows, not money and status but, rather, self-fulfillment, interpersonal satisfactions, and security receive
the greatest emphasis. If we consider those who selected
various values as their "first choices," we find that 27
percent of the students considered "an opportunity to use my
special abilities or aptitudes" most important and 10 percent
chose "permit me to be creative and original." Thus, nearly
three-eighths of the students placed the strongest stress on
the use of their innate or acquired potentialities in work.
In addition, a sixth stressed the importance of interpersonal
satisfactions—seven percent choosing "give me an opportunity
to work with people rather than things" and 10 percent "give
me an opportunity to be helpful to others." Security also
looms as an occupational gratification of great importance in
the eyes of the student, for nearly one-fourth (24 percent)
checked "enable me to look forward to a stable, secure future."
A relatively small proportion gave top priority to money and
status; 10 percent chose "provide me with a chance to earn a
good deal of money" and two percent selected "give me social
status and prestige."

Since students tend to consider more than one value as
important to them in making an occupational choice, the question arises whether certain major "value-orientations" or
"value-foci" can be distinguished from these results. One
way to examine this problem is to note whether people who
considered one value highly important to them also tended to
consider another specific value important. In order to examine this question, we have computed a coefficient of association, Q, between every pair of values.[4] The three highest
positive relationships, using the coefficient of association,
are the following:

1. "Opportunity to work with people rather than things"
and "opportunity to be helpful to others" (Q = +.580). This
might be called the "people-oriented" value complex. Respondents selecting these values tend to view work largely as
an opportunity for obtaining the gratifications to be derived
from interpersonal relations.

2. "Chance to earn a good deal of money" and "give me social status and prestige" (Q = +.594). We will refer to this
as the "extrinsic reward-oriented" value complex. Respondents
selecting these values tend to view work in *instrumental* terms;

Table 1
Ranking of "Requirements for Ideal Job or Career"
by 4,585 College Students

"Consider to what extent a job or career would have to satisfy each of these requirements before you could consider it IDEAL"	Most Important (H1)	Highly Important* (H)	Medium Importance (M)	Little or No Importance, Irrelevant, or Distasteful (L)
"Provide an opportunity to use my special abilities or aptitudes"	27%	78%	20%	2%
"Provide me with a chance to earn a good deal of money"	10	39	48	13
"Permit me to be creative and original"	10	48	39	13
"Give me social status and prestige"	2	26	53	21
"Give me an opportunity to work with people rather than things"	7	44	36	20
"Enable me to look forward to a stable, secure future"	24	61	31	8
"Leave me relatively free of supervision by others"	3	38	48	14
"Give me a chance to exercise leadership"	4	32	53	15
"Provide me with adventure"	1	16	40	44
"Give me an opportunity to be helpful to others"	10	43	44	13

* Students first ranked the values as highly important (H) and then ranked one of the values as most important (H1). Thus, all H1's are also counted as H's. All students checked each value either as high (H), medium (M), or low (L) in importance. Thus, H, M, and L for each value equals the total sample, or 100 percent. In addition, H1 for all values equals 100 percent.

they tend to emphasize the rewards to be obtained *for* work, rather than the gratifications to be derived *from* work.

3. "Permit me to be creative and original" and "opportunity to use my special abilities or aptitudes," (Q = +.470). This might be called the "self-expression-oriented" value complex. Respondents selecting these values tend to view work chiefly as an end in itself (a *goal* value), as an opportunity for expressing their talents and creative potentialities.

In other words, when confronted with the prospect of making an occupational choice, one type of student tends to ask: What rewards will I get for my work? A second type poses the question: Will it be a challenging, creative experience? And a third type inquires: Will I enjoy working with the people? Given these different questions, as we shall see, the occupational choices will vary considerably.

Psychological Distance between Occupational Values

While it is possible to distinguish certain broad occupational value-orientations, there is reason to believe that these value-orientations are not entirely separate and distinct but, rather, link into one another in a fairly orderly chain of values. This introduces the possibility of ordering these values along some sort of value spectrum; the distance between any two points on this spectrum might be considered the "psychological distance" between the occupational values.

The concept of psychological distance can be explained best by an example. In mass communications research, it is found that there is a strong positive relationship between listening to classical music and listening to semiclassical music; between listening to semiclassical music and to popular music; between listening to popular and to hillbilly music. But there is only a weak relationship between listening to classical and hillbilly music and a somewhat less weak relationship between semiclassical and hillbilly music. This suggests that hillbilly music is psychologically most distant from classical music, since few listeners to one type of music listen to the other.[5] Similar measures of cultural distance have been developed in studies of overlapping magazine readership.[6]

This approach can be applied to the study of the psychological proximity or distance among values. Since an individual may consider more than one value highly important, it may be possible to establish a measure of psychological distance among these values, such that we know that a person holding one value will be more likely to hold a second, less likely to hold a third, and so on. For this purpose, it is necessary to utilize our data on overlapping choices.

How can these values be ordered so that each occupational value, like a link in a chain, will be most likely to be related to the values adjacent to it and decreasingly likely to be related to values increasing in distance from it? In this case, we will deal only with the three major value-orientations, including "security," which logically falls into the "extrinsic-reward-oriented" category, and omit the minor value alternatives of freedom, adventure, and leadership.

On the basis of the values matrix shown in Table 2, it appears possible to establish the following values sequence:

1. Permit me to be creative and original.
2. Use my special abilities and aptitudes.
3. Permit me to be helpful to others.
4. Work with people rather than things.
5. Give me status and prestige.
6. Chance to earn a good deal of money.
7. Stable, secure future.

This means that "creative" (1) is positively related to "abilities" (2), "abilities" is positively related to "helpful" (3), "helpful" is positively related to "people" (4), and so on. However, "creative" (1) is very *negatively* related to "security" (7), which is psychologically most distant from it. The larger the gap between any two numbers, the less is an individual likely to want to satisfy both values.[7]

Table 2
Overlapping Values and Psychological Distance
(N = 4,585)

	Creative	Abilities	Helpful	People	Status	Money	Security
Creative & original	-	+.470	+.140	-.078	+.007	-.177	-.386
Abilities & aptitudes	+.470	-	+.105	-.126	-.107	-.141	-.199
Helpful to others	+.140	+.105	-	+.580	+.002	-.336	+.073
Work with people	-.078	-.126	+.580	-	+.245	-.126	+.123
Status & prestige	+.007	-.107	+.002	+.245	-	+.594	+.331
Good deal of money	-.177	-.141	-.336	-.126	+.594	-	+.342
Secure future	-.386	-.199	+.073	+.123	+.331	+.342	-

This continuum of psychological distance, it may be noted, ranges from the "self-expression" values to the "people-oriented" values to the "extrinsic-reward" values. The sequence noted above enables us to see at a glance the degree of probable mutual exclusion and inclusion of various occupational value alternatives. The more distant people are on this scale, the more radically opposed are their occupational values likely to be. The strongest value difference is between those who emphasize the satisfactions they will get *from* the work itself (work itself as a *goal* value) and those who focus on the rewards they hope to be given *for* the work they do (work as an *instrumental* value).

These results may be relevant to the work of the vocational counsellor. If the vocational counsellor feels that an individual cannot satisfy a particular occupational value in his work, he might consider the advisability of suggesting an occupation in which a psychologically contiguous, rather than remote, value may be satisfied.

Money and Security

Before considering the selection of values by people choosing different occupations, it is interesting to examine the relationship between two particular values—the desire for money and the desire for security. Traditionally, it has been considered part of the American value system for young men to aspire to monetary success. Various qualities were considered essential for the attainment of this goal—vision, daring, initiative, a willingness to take risks, etc. During the course of the depression, however, a counterideology became more prominent—the value of security. Under the stress of economic anxiety, many people gave up their interest in striving after big money and concentrated their attention on getting a steady secure job. The opposition of these two values was reflected to some extent in the conflicting political ideologies of laissez-faire vs. the welfare state.

It is therefore particularly interesting to observe in our data that money and security, which have traditionally been considered polar opposites as occupational values, are, on the contrary, psychologically close together. The coefficient of association between money and security is +.342, indicating a tendency to accept or reject both values together. In addition, these two values are contiguous on the psychological distance scale; this means that people who choose money or security tend to *reject* other values in a common fashion (e. g., the self-expression values). Finally, on the basis of a weighted average, we ranked each occupation in terms of the average emphasis placed on the value of money and on the average emphasis placed on security. The rank order coefficient of correlation between the two lists of occupations, using the Spearman formula, was +.705.

In terms of the total range of occupational value alternatives, then, the conflict of the college man does not seem to be a question of money *versus* security; rather, it appears likely, many people want money *in order* to have security.

These two values appear to be part of a common value orientation which stresses the extrinsic rewards of work.

The Distribution of Value-Complexes among Occupations

If values play a role in determining one's occupational
choice, then we would expect people planning to enter different occupations to vary in their values. And, indeed, this
variation turns out to be wide and tends to be consistent
with the structure of the occupation.

By means of a weighted average,[8] we ranked each occupation
in terms of the emphasis which people planning to enter the
field placed on the three major value-complexes (self-expression-oriented, people-oriented, and extrinsic-reward-oriented).
As Table 3 shows, students planning to enter the fields of
architecture, art, journalism, or drama are most concerned
with creativity or the use of their talents in their work,
followed by natural scientists and social scientists. The
field most strongly de-emphasizing self-expression in work
are the business occupations of sales-promotion, hotel management, and real estate or finance.

The "people-oriented" value complex, as Table 4 indicates,
is most strongly stressed by students planning to enter social
work, medicine, teaching, social science, and personnel work.
It is quite obvious in this case that the occupational value
and the nature of the work are meaningfully related, for each
of these occupations involves work for, with, or about other
people.

The relationship between the structure of the occupation
and the values selected is also revealed by the fact that the
occupations which place the *least* emphasis on "people-oriented"
values are natural science, engineering, farming, art, and
architecture. This is to be expected, for work in these
fields plainly embraces, as structural imperatives, the manipulation of physical matter or impersonal problems. The relationship between the occupational value and the nature of the
work rather clearly suggests that what the student wants out
of his work delimits and channels the range of occupations in
which he might be interested.

If this is so, then it is not surprising that people planning to enter real estate or finance, sales-promotion, hotel
management, law, advertising, and business should place the
greatest stress on the extrinsic rewards of money, status, and
security (Table 5). Considerably less stress is placed on
these values by social workers, teachers, natural scientists,
farmers, and social scientists (although farmers and natural

Table 3
Occupations Ranked According to Weighted Average Score
on "Self-Expression-Oriented" Value Complex

Occupations	Weighted Average of "Self-Expression-Oriented" Values	Total Cases
Architecture	5.78	(88)
Journalism-Drama	5.44	(70)
Art	5.42	(193)
Natural science	4.83	(300)
Social science	4.70	(23)
Advertising-Public relations	4.68	(72)
Engineering	4.65	(553)
Teaching	4.52	(400)
Farming	3.99	(108)
Law	3.98	(318)
Social work	3.81	(70)
Medicine	3.76	(691)
Business (unspecified)	3.71	(453)
Government	3.69	(152)
Personnel	3.59	(134)
Real estate-Finance	3.52	(105)
Hotel-Food	3.23	(40)
Sales-promotion	3.20	(135)
Total Weighted Average	(4.21)	(3,905)

scientists are highly concerned with security).

It is evident that these various occupations have certain technical or structural imperatives which permit the satisfaction of particular values. Self-expression is the essence of artistic work, and working with people is indispensable in social work. The importance of this fact for social motivation is that in a society with diverse occupations capable of satisfying many values, a greater degree of matching between values and the technical requirements of the occupation becomes possible. This matching may contribute importantly to work motivation, thereby extracting a greater share of the creative energies of men in the society in their work.

The fact that such a wide range of values may be satisfied in work may also be considered from another point of view. While there is sometimes an off-hand tendency to assume that people work because of the money or status or security it will bring them, a little reflection makes obvious a fact revealed by our data, namely, that many place greater stress on the satisfactions involved in doing the job itself, in ex-

Table 4
Occupations Ranked According to Weighted Average Score
on "People-Oriented" Value Complex

Occupations	Weighted Average of "People-Oriented" Values	Total Cases
Social work	5.33	(70)
Medicine	4.12	(691)
Teaching	4.06	(400)
Social science	3.78	(23)
Personnel	3.64	(134)
Government	3.41	(152)
Law	3.26	(318)
Sales-promotion	3.01	(135)
Advertising-Public relations	3.00	(72)
Real estate-Finance	2.98	(105)
Hotel-Food	2.85	(40)
Journalism-Drama	2.83	(70)
Business-unspecified	2.65	(453)
Architecture	2.53	(88)
Art	2.51	(193)
Farming	2.14	(108)
Engineering	1.95	(553)
Natural science	1.79	(300)
Total Weighted Average	(3.07)	(3,905)

pressing their creative potentialities, or in the pleasures
of interpersonal interaction which is a part of their work.

Viewed from the perspective of the total economic structure, this fact may represent an important windfall for society. Any society has a limited (hence, scarce) amount of
material goods (or money) and prestige to distribute to its
members. However, the technical structure of many functional
occupations is of such a nature that the very activity itself
provides self-expressive gratifications. In other words,
some of the inducements are "built in" to the occupation.
Consequently, if the work is enjoyable in itself, it need not
be so heavily rewarded. Thus, relatively small material rewards may induce scientists or artists or social workers to
invest great amounts of intellectual and emotional effort in
their work, thereby performing their occupational functions
at a relatively high level of efficiency and low social cost,
whereas much larger rewards would be required to elicit this
degree of involvement in work which is less inherently satisfying.

Table 5
Occupations Ranked According to Weighted Average Score on "Extrinsic-Reward-Oriented" Value Complex; and Weighted Average for "Security"

Occupations	Weighted Average on "Extrinsic-Reward" Values	Weighted Average— "Security"	Total Cases
Real estate-Finance	3.64	2.30	(105)
Hotel-Food	3.58	2.60	(40)
Sales-promotion	3.53	2.39	(135)
Law	3.34	2.16	(318)
Advertising	3.21	2.18	(72)
Business (unspecified)	3.19	2.30	(453)
Personnel	3.09	2.11	(134)
Medicine	2.58	2.16	(691)
Engineering	2.55	2.24	(553)
Government	2.55	1.84	(152)
Art	2.54	1.51	(193)
Journalism-Drama	2.50	1.39	(70)
Architecture	2.40	1.76	(88)
Social science	2.30	1.83	(23)
Farming	2.13	2.31	(108)
Natural science	2.07	2.16	(300)
Teaching	1.96	1.95	(400)
Social work	1.33	1.29	(70)
Total Weighted Average	(2.66)	(2.10)	(3905)

The Mutual Interaction of Occupational Values and Choices

While there is a characteristic tendency for people wanting to enter certain occupations to hold particular value-
orientations, Tables 3, 4, and 5 also reveal that there are
many people whose values and occupational choices are rather
inconsistent; they select values and choices which generally
do not go together. If the student comes to recognize this
as a conflict, we might expect him in the course of time to
change either his values or his occupational choice so that
they would agree with each other. Is there any evidence indicating an increasing psychological consistency between values and choices as the student advances in his college career?

Data on changes of values and choices are not available for
the total sample, but there were 944 students at Cornell who
filled out questionnaires both in 1950 and in 1952. Since the
questions on values and choices were phrased identically in

both studies, it was possible to observe whether consistency increased during the two-year span.

Let us take, for example, Table 4, which ranks occupations in terms of the emphasis placed on "people-oriented" values. If we arbitrarily consider the top half of the list as "people-oriented" occupations (or PO Occ) and the bottom half as "non-people-oriented" occupations (or NPO Occ), then we can observe whether the relationship between the choice of these occupations and the selection of the "people-oriented" values increases among the same people during this two-year period. The results are shown in Table 6. ("People-oriented" values will be called "PO" values and "non-people-oriented" values, "NPO" values.)

Table 6
Relationship between Occupational Values
and Occupational Choices in 1950 and 1952

Choices	1950 Values			Choices	1952 Values		
	PO	NPO	Total		PO	NPO	Total
PO Occ	226	89	315	PO Occ	226	66	292
NPO Occ	166	231	397	NPO Occ	154	266	420
Total	392	320	712	Total	380	332	712

It will be noted that in 1950 there were 89 people with NPO values who chose PO occupations, and 166 people with PO values who chose NPO occupations. In terms of the general relationship between occupational values and occupational choices, these 255 people were the psychologically inconsistent group, and constituted 36 percent of the panel members.[9] By 1952, however, there were 66 NPO values with PO occupations and 154 people with PO values choosing NPO occupations. In other words, there were now 220 inconsistent people, or 31 percent of the sample. The percentage differences between "inconsistents" on the two waves are statistically significant at the .05 level. Another way of expressing this trend is to note that in 1950 the coefficient of association between occupational choices and occupational values was $Q = +.559$, whereas by 1952 the coefficient of association had increased to $Q = +.711$.

There is thus a significant trend toward increased psychological consistency, although it is not a large one.

The trend noted above, however, does not reveal the complete picture of turnover. In order to observe all the combinations of occupational choices and occupational values in

1950 and 1952, it is necessary to present the data within the framework of a 16-fold table (Table 7).

Table 7
"People-Oriented" Occupational Values and Occupational Choices in 1950 and 1952

Occupational Values and Choices, 1950	Occupational Values and Choices 1952				
	PO Occ. PO Val.	PO Occ. NPO Val.	NPO Occ. PO Val.	NPO Occ. NPO Val.	Total
PO Occ.-PO Val.	163	15	30	18	226
PO Occ.-NPO Val.	21	29	8	31	89
NPO Occ.-PO Val.	36	8	73	49	166
NPO Occ.-NPO Val.	6	14	43	168	231
Total	226	66	154	266	712

Let us examine the people who were inconsistent in 1950. There were 255 such people, 89 PO Occ.-NPO Val's and 166 NPO Occ.-PO Val's. These people might behave in one of three possible ways. The first possibility would be that they might change either their occupational choices or their occupational values so that they now held a psychologically consistent position. It turns out that, of those 255 originally inconsistent people, 137, or 54 percent, had now become consistent. The second possibility would be that these people would maintain their original inconsistency, changing neither their occupational choices nor occupational values. It turns out that 102 people, or 40 percent of these respondents, did so. Finally, it is possible that these inconsistent people might change both values and choices, thereby achieving an inconsistent position which was the diametric opposite of their original position. This turns out to be the rarest phenomenon of all, with only 16 cases, or six percent, manifesting this behavior. There is thus an evident tendency for people with psychologically inconsistent positions to become more consistent with the lapse of time.

This change is in striking contrast to those who were originally consistent; these people tended to maintain their same consistent position. Of the 457 consistent people in 1950, 331, or 72 percent, maintained the same consistency in 1952; 102, or 22 percent, became inconsistent; and 24, or five percent, changed to the opposite pole of consistency.

It is thus evident that people who are originally consistent tend to *remain* consistent. However, it may be noted that there are relatively few "complete reversals," *i. e.*, inconsistents who change both choice and values to become inconsistent in the opposite way, or consistents who change both choice and values to become consistent in the opposite way. If changes occur, these are usually changes of either choice or values, but rarely both.

Having noted that occupational choice and occupational values increased in consistency between 1950 and 1952, the question which logically arises is: Is this increased consistency achieved by people changing their values to accord with their occupational choices, or is it achieved by people changing their choices to accord with their values?

A new method for analyzing such mutual interaction has been suggested by Paul F. Lazarsfeld.[10] Let us take those people who, both in 1950 and 1952, selected the *same* values (the "value-constants"); if they changed their occupational choices, did they tend to change them in a manner consistent with these values? Then let us take those people who, both in 1950 and 1952, selected the same type of occupation (the "occupational choice-constants"); if they changed their values, did they tend to change them in a manner consistent with these occupational choices? It would then be possible to ask: Which factor appeared to produce the greater change in the other? This might then tell us, at least in a rough way, whether values or occupational choices were "stronger" in influencing the other (Table 8).

Table 8
Mutual Interaction of Values and Occupational Choices

	A				B		
	Values				**Occupational Choices**		
	1950	PO Val	NPO Val		1950	PO Occ	NPO Occ
	1952	PO Val	NPO Val		1952	PO Occ	NPO Occ
Choices 1950	1952			Values 1950	1952		
PO Occ-NPO Occ		30	31	PO Val-NPO Val		15	49
NPO Occ-PO Occ		36(57%)	14(31%)	NPO Val-PO Val		21(58%)	43(47%)
		N (66)	(45)			N (36)	(92)

It may be noted that 57 percent of the students selecting people-oriented values on both waves changed to people-oriented occupations, compared with 31 percent of those who did not select these values, a difference of 26 percent. On the other hand, 58 percent of those who chose people-oriented occupations switched to people-oriented values, compared with 47 percent of those who did not choose one of these occupations, a difference of only 11 percent. *This would suggest that values have a greater effect on change of occupational choice than the other way around.* The over-all pattern of this mutual interaction is to reduce the conflict between values and occupational choices.

The Impact of Occupational Choices on Values

The fact that values influence occupational choices is in agreement with the common-sense notion that if a person wants something he will look for an occupation in which he thinks he can get it. But the data in Table 8 (B), indicating that occupational choices influence values, inevitably raise the question of the causal relationship between these two factors. We observe a relationship between a value and an occupational choice and we say, for example, that one reason a man wants to become a businessman is that he wants to make a good deal of money. Nevertheless, the fact that many people change their values to agree with their occupational choices suggests that the opposite statement, which on a common-sense level may appear absurd, may actually be true; namely, that he wants money *because* he has decided to become a businessman. How might this come about? Let us say that a student is the son of a successful businessman, and it is assumed by all concerned that he will take over the business, which has been in the family for several generations, when his father retires. He knows that, in general, there are many values which can be satisfied in one's work—creativity, adventure, independence, enjoyable personal relationships, money, status, etc. It will probably occur to him at some time that he would very much like to exercise his artistic potentialities at work. He may thus be caught in a conflict: he wants to enter the family business, he wants to exercise his artistic potentialities, and he feels that as a businessman he cannot use these potentialities. We would assume, therefore, that he would decide against business and would switch, let us say, to art or music. But another possibility must also be considered. He may have his heart set on becoming a businessman; the structure of his self-image and his entire future may be bound up in taking over the business; he may find the prospect of leading an "artist's life" disagreeable; and so on. Thereupon he may come to the conclusion that, after all, a desire to be artistic is very unrealistic, an adolescent fantasy; that artists are queer people who can never lead normal lives; that artists are never recognized in their own lifetimes; and that, when you really think of it, there are a great many advantages in having money—a nice house, car, vacations, security. He may start ruminating on the virtues of money, which grow increasingly glittering in his mind. And, it is clear, he can make a good deal of money in the family business. Thus the conflict is resolved, and it can properly be said that the occupational choice has determined the value. If this were a mere rationalization, of course, then the conflict would continue beneath the surface; however, in many cases, we submit, the value actually does change to accord with the choice.

In other words, we ordinarily take for granted the following obvious psychological sequence: a person first wants something and then he acts to get it (the action is a result of the value). In some cases, however, the opposite pattern occurs: *the person wants something because he has acted to get it.*

This principle, as it applies to occupational decisions, might be stated in more general terms. For certain sociological reasons—the individual's social milieu, the positions in the social structure of his family and friends, his sex status, his various membership groups—the student is directed toward the "voluntary" selection of an occupation. Having chosen the field, he is likely to incorporate into his present self-image aspects of his future occupational status—he is a "future doctor," "future teacher," "future engineer." In the course of time, he develops a picture of the attitudes, values, and behavior which are appropriate for a member of this occupation (*e. g.*; a doctor should want to alleviate the sufferings of mankind, an artist should want to exercise his creative potentialities). This image of his *future* occupational status is likely to influence the student's *present* attitudes, values, and behavior; he may start to think and behave in a way which he believes will be appropriate when he actually enters occupational practice. This is the process which Merton has called *anticipatory socialization.* The occupational status *still to be occupied* influences the *current* attitudes, values, and behavior of the individual. Thus, in addition to people choosing an occupation in order to satisfy a value, they may choose a value because they consider it appropriate for the occupational status they expect to fill in the future.

This has interesting implications for the entire analysis of values. Values are not only determinants of action, but are themselves determined by actions which are patterned on the basis of one's position in society. Both values and choices tend to determine one another, and both tend to change in the direction of greater mutual consistency, thereby leading to reduction of conflict.

CHAPTER III

FAITH IN PEOPLE AND OCCUPATIONAL ATTITUDES

The Importance of Interpersonal Factors

Occupational activity is more than just a matter of doing one's job; it is a social system as well. The businessman not only has to cope with inventories or production; he must also deal with customers and employees. The teacher must do more than master physics or English literature; he must also master relationships with students, colleagues, and administrators. The aspiring lawyer who has a thorough knowledge of torts, contracts, etc., does not automatically achieve success; his future depends very importantly on the impression he will make on clients, judges, and jurors. Interpersonal relations are thus tightly woven into the fabric of occupational activity. Relationships of employer and employee, professional and client, salesman and customer, producer and consumer, teacher and student, manager and technician, officer and men, foreman and workers, actor and audience, partner and partner, colleague and colleague—all these involve interpersonal relationships and skills of various sorts.

While our respondents by no means underestimate the importance of the technical aspects of work, a large number of them are keenly aware of the fact that a job means *work with people*. Many of them place strong stress on the interpersonal values they hope to satisfy in their work, for, as we noted earlier, forty-five percent of the respondents emphasized that working with people (rather than things) was an important aspect of their ideal jobs; and forty-three percent insisted on the importance of being "helpful to others." In addition, the students consider interpersonal skills—the ability to get along with people, to handle them, to influence them--extremely important for occupational success. In many cases, such skills are considered more important than native talents or monetary resources.

Faith in People and Occupational Choice

If interpersonal relations are viewed as an important aspect of one's career, then it is relevant to consider how
interpersonal attitudes may influence the individual's perception of his career. Perhaps the broadest and most basic
interpersonal attitude might be one's view of human nature,
or "faith in people." By this concept we refer to the individual's degree of confidence in the trustworthiness, hones-
ty, goodness, generosity, and brotherliness of the mass of
men. A scale of faith in people, consisting of five items
reflecting the manifest content of the concept, was con-
structed, using the Guttman method;[1] the reproducibility was
.92. The items used were the following:

(1) Some people say that most people can be trusted.
Others say you can't be too careful in your dealings
with people. How do you feel about it?
____ Most people can be trusted.
____ You can't be too careful.
(2) Would you say that most people are more inclined
to help others, or more inclined to look out for themselves?
____ To help others.
____ To look out for themselves.
(3) If you don't watch yourself, people will take advantage of you.   A D ?[2]
(4) No one is going to care much what happens to you,
when you get right down to it.   A D ?
(5) Human nature is fundamentally cooperative.
                                                   A D ?

"Positive" responses were those indicating *absence*[3] of "faith
in people." The five items, of course, yielded six groups.
There are many occupations in which attitudes toward other
human beings would not appear to be a relevant factor in
choice. For example, it is hard to imagine why an individual
who distrusts or dislikes others should choose or reject, *on
this basis alone*, the field of engineering rather than, let
us say, architecture or physical science. In certain specific cases, however, one's feelings about interpersonal relations are clearly of importance. In social work, for example,
it is implicit in the technical requirements of the field
that the practitioner have an emotionally positive feeling
toward others.
     In fact, as Table 9 shows, the three occupations with the
greatest proportion of those with high faith in people are

social work, personnel work, and teaching; the occupations
with the lowest proportion are sales-promotion, business-
finance, and advertising-public relations. It may be noted
that both sets of occupations involve working with people
but that the *quality* of the interpersonal relationship differs basically. The relationship of the social worker,
personnel worker, and teacher to the people with whom they
primarily deal tends to be a *helpful* one (concern with the
interests of the other);[4] the relationship of the advertiser,
businessman, and salesman tends to be a self-interested one
(concern with the interests of the self). It would appear
that there is some tendency for those with different degrees
of faith in human nature to select occupational areas involving a *quality* of interpersonal relations consistent with this
attitude.

Table 9
Occupations Ranked in Order of Faith in People

Occupation	High Faith Percent	Medium and Low Faith Percent	Total, 100%
Social work	62	38	(26)
Personnel	59	41	(43)
Teaching	56	44	(146)
Science	51	49	(103)
Government	50	50	(57)
Farming	45	55	(106)
Art	43	57	(63)
Hotel	41	59	(63)
Medicine	40	60	(128)
Journalism-Drama	39	61	(23)
Architecture	39	61	(36)
Law	39	61	(54)
Engineering	36	64	(282)
Advertising-Public Relations	36	64	(22)
Business-Finance	34	66	(132)
Sales-Promotion	22	78	(37)

It may be noted that social work and teaching are traditionally women's fields whereas men are more likely to enter
business; women also express a higher degree of faith in
people. When we consider men and women separately, however,
the relationship between faith in people and occupational
choice remains substantially unchanged.

In summary, it seems reasonable to say that while faith in
people will hardly ever completely determine an individual's

choice of a specific occupation, it may clearly attract
people to a certain *set* of occupations or general occupational *area* and repel them from other occupational areas. For
example, those who have high faith in people may well be de-
terred from entering business or sales-promotion because they
feel the work requirements run counter to their basic feelings about others. Similarly, a person may stay away from
the field of social work if he feels that a social worker
should extend warmth and human sympathy to people.

Faith in People and Occupational Values

    In noting that those students with high faith in people
were more likely to select occupations which were characterized by a "helpful" system of interpersonal relations, and
that those with low faith chose "self-interested" occupations, we were forced to infer, on the basis of our general
knowledge of the interpersonal relations obtaining in these
occupations, what interpersonal factors helped to account for
this choice. It is possible to study the relationship between faith in people and the interpersonal factors in work
more directly through the study of occupational values.
    What is the relationship between the way the individual
feels about humanity and what he would like to get out of his
job? As we would expect, those with high faith in people are
most likely to want to satisfy "people-oriented" occupational
values; *i. e.*, they want to work with people rather than
things and they want the chance to be helpful to others
(Table 10).

Table 10
Faith in People and "People-Oriented" Occupational Values

"People-Oriented" Occupational Values	Faith in People					
	High Faith 1	2	3	4	5	Low Faith 6
	(213)	(427)	(356)	(245)	(162)	(72)
First choice—"Work with people rather than things"	19%	17%	7%	8%	7%	11%
First choice—"Helpful to others"	14	9	7	6	9	3
Lowest value—"Work with people rather than things"	17	21	23	27	27	36
Lowest value—"Helpful to others"	9	13	16	23	26	34

The satisfaction of an occupational value thus appears to be a specific expression of a more general value complex revolving about one's views of humanity. There is also additional evidence[5] showing that faith in people is strongly related to prejudice toward minority groups, attitudes toward democratic political principles, and even attitudes toward international relations. These findings underscore the importance of seeking in social research for certain basic orientations which help to account for attitudes and behavior in a wide variety of life situations.

To return to the question of occupational values, we find that whereas those with high faith in people stress *interpersonal* occupational values, those with low faith tend, relatively, to choose an *impersonal* value, namely, "the chance to earn a good deal of money." Almost one-fifth of the latter valued the opportunity to earn a good deal of money compared with only two percent of the former. Conversely, 25 percent of those with low faith, compared with eight percent of those with high faith, considered this value irrelevant (Table 11).

Table 11
Faith in People and Money as an Occupational Value

Occupational Value "...chance to earn a good deal of money"	Faith in People					
	High Faith 1	2	3	4	5	Low Faith 6
	(213)	(427)	(356)	(245)	(162)	(72)
First choice	2%	6%	7%	12%	16%	19%
Low choice	25	16	11	12	9	8

The influence of interpersonal factors on occupational choice is particularly clear when we consider the combined influence of faith in people and values. For example, we would expect those people selecting people-oriented occupational values and having high faith in people to be more likely than others to choose an occupation which is especially devoted to helping or improving others in a friendly interpersonal context. Conversely, we would expect those with low faith in people who seek an impersonal value, such as money, to select an occupation in which the interpersonal relations are likely to be of a self-interested nature (in the sense of guiding the actions of others in channels promoting one's own ends). We will consider the "helpful" occupations to be teaching, social work, and personnel, and the "self-interested" occupations to be business, real estate-finance, sales-promotion, and advertising-public relations (Table 12).

Table 12
Faith in People-Occupational Values
and Choice of Occupational Area

Selection of Occupational Area	Those with High Faith Who Select "People-Oriented" Values First Choice	Misanthropes Who Select "Money" as High Choice
"Helpful" occupations	50%	8%
"Self-interested" occupations	3	23
Others	47	69
N	(62)	(106)

Exactly one-half of those with high faith in people who selected "people-oriented" values chose one of the "helpful" occupations compared with only 8 percent of the misanthropes selecting "money" as an occupational value. Conversely, only 3 percent of the former group, compared with nearly eight times that proportion of members of the latter group (23 percent) selected one of the self-interested occupations. The pattern of avoidance is perhaps even more striking than the pattern of selection. Ninety-seven percent of the former group avoided one of the "self-interested" occupations, and 92 percent of the latter group avoided one of the "helpful" occupations. Phrasing these findings in predictive terms, we may say that an individual who likes and wishes to work with others has a good chance (50 percent) of selecting one of the "helpful" occupations (teaching, social work, and personnel) and an extremely slim chance (3 percent) of choosing one of the "self-interested" occupations (business, real estate-finance, sales-promotion, and advertising-public relations). Conversely, a person who does not trust others and selects the relatively "impersonal" value of money as a requirement for his ideal job is very unlikely to choose one of the "helpful" occupations (8 percent); on the other hand, this does not necessarily mean that he will select one of the "self-interested" occupations, since less than one-fourth (23 percent) do so. In the latter case, then, the influence of interpersonal attitudes and values would appear to operate more clearly to keep these people *out* of certain occupational areas than to draw them *into* certain occupational areas.

Faith in People and Attitudes toward Occupational Practice

If interpersonal relations are actually a significant factor in the world of work, then it is easy to imagine how the
individual's fundamental feelings about human nature might
influence his behavior in that area. Take an extreme hypothetical example of an individual who feels that people cannot be trusted. This person, if he had partners, might tend
to watch them like a hawk; he might be cautious about extend-
ing credit, requiring more than the customary amount of col-
lateral; he might be constantly on his guard against others
cheating him; he might be dubious about hard-luck stories;
he might be more reluctant to help others in business difficulties; and so on. An adequate understanding of economic
and occupational performance must take into account at some
level variables such as faith in human nature.

We do not know how our relatively misanthropic respondents will behave when they actually go to work, but we do
have evidence regarding the attitudes they are likely to
bring to their jobs. Simply expressed, they will hold relatively unscrupulous and cynical attitudes.

It is consistent with the misanthrope's view of human
nature that he tends to view the world of work as something
of a jungle, where victory is achieved by any means, fair or
foul. For example, our respondents were asked to agree or
disagree with the statement, "In order to get ahead these
days...you can't afford to be squeamish about the means you
use." Most respondents disagreed with the statement; but,
as Table 13 indicates, whereas 10 percent of those with the
highest faith in people agreed, fully 57 percent of those
with the least faith agreed. It certainly seems possible
that if an individual considers the world of work a "tough"
place, in which the highest rewards go to the unscrupulous,
he will decide to be tough and unscrupulous in his own occupational dealings.

Table 13
Faith in People and Willingness to Use Unscrupulous Means

"You can't afford to be squeamish..."	Faith in People					
	High Faith 1	2	3	4	5	Low Faith 6
Agree	10%	8%	12%	23%	34%	57%
Undecided	13	11	12	10	10	7
Disagree	78	81	76	67	55	36
N	(231)	(438)	(374)	(259)	(173)	(75)

Individuals with low faith in people are also relatively likely to express the idea that the use of illegitimate means of achieving success is a widespread social phenomenon. Cornell students were asked to agree or disagree with the following statement: "It's who you know more than what you know that counts these days " This statement expresses a belief in the efficacy of "contacts" or "inside dealing" as means of success and a cynical denial of the relevance of ability.

Table 14
Faith in People and Belief that
"It's Who You Know that Counts"

"Who you know more than what you know"	High Faith					Low Faith
	1	2	3	4	5	6
Agree	12%	17%	26%	29%	46%	59%
Undecided	20	18	18	18	13	7
Disagree	68	64	56	53	40	35
N	(227)	(426)	(366)	(258)	(174)	(75)

The differences appearing in Table 14 are so sharp as to arouse the suspicion that we are tapping the same dimension. However, the manifest content of the two variables is clearly different—the one dealing with faith in people, the other dealing with a belief in an effective means of success. Less than one-eighth of those with high faith in people agreed that "It's who you know that counts" compared with nearly three-fifths of the misanthropes. As faith in people decreases, the proportion agreeing with the statement increases regularly.

In sum, knowledge of an individual's degree of faith in people may serve as a valuable indicator of his probable occupational orientation. On the basis of these data, we might very well expect the misanthropes to be relatively manipulative when they enter their chosen fields of endeavor. Whether circumstances will allow them to translate their attitudes into action is a question that cannot be answered at this point; but that they are predisposed to behave in this fashion, relative to those with high faith in people, is evident from the data.

To summarize, we may say that the world of work appears to be viewed in part as a system of human interaction, and that the way an individual feels about people influences his per-

ception of his career--the values he hopes to satisfy, the
field he chooses, and the means for achieving success which
he finds acceptable. Otherwise stated, work involves people,
and the way one feels about people influences the way one
feels about work.

Faith in People and Success-Orientation

Analysts of the American value system have emphasized the
importance of "success," of social mobility, as a central
social value. In the middle class, at least, the individual
is encouraged to want to get ahead, to elevate himself in
the status hierarchy. For example, Middletown believes "in
being successful," say the Lynds.[6] "...a man owes it to
himself, to his family, and to society to 'succeed'...one
should be enterprising; one should try to get ahead of one's
fellows, but not 'in an underhand way.' "[7] Merton observes
that "...the (American) culture enjoins the acceptance of
three cultural axioms: First, all should strive for the
same lofty goals since these are open to all; second, present
seeming failure is but a way station to ultimate success; and
third, genuine failure consists only in the lessening or
withdrawal of ambition."[8] And in his discussion of the
American value system, Williams has noted: "First, American
culture is marked by a central stress upon personal achievement, especially secular occupational achievement. The
'success story' and the respect accorded to the self-made
man are distinctly American, if anything is. Our society...
has endorsed Horatio Alger and has glorified the rail split-
ter who becomes president."[9] This emphasis upon success has
also been noted by Cuber and Harper,[10] Margaret Mead,[11]
Myrdal,[12] Fromm,[13] Horney,[14] and others.

An attempt to test this general assumption regarding the
value of success in the middle class was made by asking our
respondents the following question: "How important to you,
personally, is it to get ahead in life?" Eighty-eight percent of the student sample considered it either very important (45 percent) or fairly important (43 percent) to get
ahead, whereas only 10 percent considered it not very important, and only 2 percent checked it as very unimportant.
Although these results do not reflect a universally *burning*
desire for success (only 45 per cent considered it *very* important), the value of success does appear to be generally
embraced by the members of our student sample. This finding
naturally leads to the further question: "Why do some people

consider it more important to get ahead than others?"

An attempt to provide a complete answer to this question
cannot be undertaken here. It is interesting, however, to
consider whether faith in people is implicated in the intensity of one's desire for success. Horney has observed that
an individual who has a basic hatred of people often develops
a desire to dominate them, control them, master them, establish his superiority over them. In a world which is viewed
as a jungle, inhabited by predatory beasts, the only safety
lies in getting so much power and strength that one is in-
vulnerable to the attacks of others.[15] Such an attitude
fits in neatly with the culturally defined value of success,
which involves a competitive struggle for superiority. It
was therefore hypothesized that part of the differential emphasis upon success could be accounted for in terms of the
individual's degree of faith in people, *i. e.*, those with
low faith in people would consider it more important to get
ahead in life than those with high faith in people. The results appear in Table 15.

Table 15
Faith in People and Desire to Get Ahead

Important to Get Ahead in Life	High Faith	Medium Faith	Low Faith
Very important	38%	49%	57%
Not very important	62	51	43
N	(673)	(618)	(251)

The fact that 57 percent of those with low faith in people
considered success very important, compared with 38 percent
of those with high faith, highlights the complexity of factors involved in striving after success. On the one hand, as
our evidence suggests, it may in part involve a desire to
master a humanity one despises. On the other hand, as
Williams has noted, success in American culture tends to be
used as a measure of achievement and as a standard of personal excellence. "Money comes to be valued not only for itself
and the goods it will buy, but also as symbolic evidence of
success and thereby of personal worth."[16] People who highly
value success in American society may simply be seeking to
demonstrate their worth in a manner highly acceptable to the
society.

We would thus expect that the impact of faith in people
upon one's desire to get ahead would tend to be strongest
upon those who are not under strong cultural pressure to be

successful. One simple fact which is overlooked surprising-
ly often in discussions of success is that the value is considered much more appropriate for men than for women. Women
are much more likely to attain a higher status through the
success of their husbands than through their own achievements.
This certainly tends to be the case among the members of our
sample; only 28 percent of the women, compared with 51 percent
of the men, considered it "very important" to get ahead in
life. We would thus expect the influence of the individual's
degree of faith in people on his success-orientation to be
greater among the women than among the men since, in the former case, this relationship is less likely to be adulterated
by a general social pressure to succeed. The results given
in Table 16 support this expectation.

Table 16
Faith in People and Desire to Get Ahead, by Sex

	Men			Women		
			Faith in People			
Important to Get Ahead	High	Medium	Low	High	Medium	Low
Very important	48%	52%	59%	19%	34%	51%
Not very important	52	48	41	81	66	49
N	(444)	(491)	(200)	(229)	(137)	(51)

Among the men, 59 percent of those with low faith in people
considered it "very important" to get ahead, compared with 52
percent of those with medium faith and 48 percent of those
with high faith. The individual's basic interpersonal attitude thus has some influence on his desire for success, but
the difference between the men with the most and the least
faith in people is only 11 percent. Among the women, however,
fully 51 percent of those with low faith in people were particularly anxious to be successful, compared with only 19
percent of those with high faith, a difference of 32 percent,
or nearly three times as great as that obtaining among the
men. This example illustrates the general point that a relationship which obtains between two variables for a total
sample may hold with different degrees of strength among various subgroups of that sample. Many men in American society,
irrespective of their attitudes toward humanity, accept the
idea that they should do their best to get ahead. Consequently, the relationship between these two variables in this population subgroup, though significant, is considerably smaller
than that among women, who are not exposed to the same degree
of cultural pressure to get ahead.

CHAPTER IV

PERSONALITY AND CAREER

What influence do personality factors have upon occupational choice? This question has been a tantalizing subject to many students of the sociology of occupations, but it has not proved easy to pin down this influence. Ginzberg and his associates have been sufficiently interested in the subject to review thoroughly the work in the area, but have been disappointed in the fruits of their labors. They conclude: "Our position...is that even though no psychological theory can adequately explain the (occupational) choice process, emotional factors are inherent in it; since relatively little is known about this fundamental relation, we strongly recommend further research."[1]

Suggestive hypotheses are plentiful, but systematic data are scarce. One might hypothesize, for example, that a person who is psychologically insecure or anxious might seek a steady, secure job; that a compulsive perfectionist might seek to attach himself to an organization requiring a rigid adherence to precise rules; that an "oral" personality might select a verbal occupation (law, teaching); that the "anal" type might seek work providing possibilities for acquisition (business); that a detached personality might select an occupation allowing him independence (art, medicine, exploration); that an extrovert might choose outgoing or exhibitionist occupations, such as acting or salesmanship; that an introvert might choose "thoughtful" or self-sufficient occupations (science, poetry); that an "authoritarian" personality might choose occupations involving a rigid system of domination, such as the army; that a sado-masochist (in Fromm's sense)[2] might select an organization involving a rigid delineation of authority; that an "other-directed" personality[3] might choose an occupation requiring sensitivity to the needs of others; that an "inner-directed" type might select an occupation in terms of a firm or rigid sense of values; and so on.

In addition to hypotheses of this sort, there are theories which seek to relate some specific aspect of childhood exper-

ience to subsequent occupational choice. Ginzberg, for example, skeptically quotes a distinguished Freudian, Ernest
Jones, to the effect that "a child, for instance, who has
conquered a sadistic love of cruelty may, when he grows up,
be a successful butcher or a distinguished surgeon according
to his capacities and opportunities... Gregory Zilboorg
tells of one of his patients whose father devoted a great
deal of time, thought, and conversation to regulating and
checking upon his children's bowel movements; the patient became a successful businessman dealing in bathroom and toilet
fixtures."[4]

Systematic tests of such hypotheses are rare. The problems of obtaining adequate indices of such complex personality types, of controlling the influence of multitudinous non-
personality factors, and of relating these personality characteristics in a specific way to occupational values and
choices are extremely complex. In the present study, we did
not delve deeply into the personality structures of our respondents, but we did utilize certain items designed to give
us a glimpse of some of their personality traits. Since the
study of this problem area is still in its bare beginnings,
it appears worthwhile to utilize the crude data available to
consider whether certain aspects of personality structure are
in some way related to occupational values and choices.

The Influence of Self-Confidence

We may begin by looking at the common-sense notion of
self-confidence. Everyone is familiar with the self-confident
type of person. He is the kind of man who strikes us as very
sure of himself; he is relatively unworried, is not hypersen-
sitive, is usually in good spirits. On the other hand, there
is another type of person—the opposite of the first—who is
constantly worried, never appears able to relax, lacks a
basic feeling of being worthwhile, constantly worries about
doing things wrong. Most people we know, of course, fit
somewhere between these two extreme types.

In an effort to determine whether our respondents could be
ranged along this hypothetical continuum, we presented them
with the following four questions:

(1) I usually don't have enough confidence in myself.

                                              A D ?[5]

(2) I get upset if someone criticizes me, no matter
who it is.   A D ?

(3) How would you say you feel most of the time—in good spirits or in low spirits?

____ Very good spirits
____ Fairly good spirits
____ Neither good nor bad
____ Fairly low spirits
____ Very low spirits

(4) Are you the sort of person who lets things worry you or don't you let things worry you?

____ Let things worry me very much
____ Let things worry me quite a bit
____ Let things worry me somewhat
____ Don't let things worry me

Empirically, these items appear to relate to one another in a meaningful pattern; using the Guttman method, they formed a reliable scale, with an index of reproducibility of .93.

If we tentatively assume that the person who gives the "positive" responses is the "self-confident" or "self-assured" type, and that the one who gives the "negative" responses is the "anxious" or "insecure" type, then the question arises: How will the individual's degree of self-confidence influence his orientation toward his career?

In the first place we find, as one would expect, that the self-confident people are more optimistic about their occupational futures. Students were asked what occupational values they hoped to satisfy in their work, and then were asked how many of these values they actually expected to satisfy. Eighty percent of the most self-confident people expected to satisfy "most of them," compared with 55 percent of the least self-assured.

Table 17
Self-Confidence and Expectation
of Satisfying Occupational Values

"Do you think the job or career you have selected as your life work will satisfy most of the requirements you marked "H", some of them, or only a few?"	Self-Confidence				
	Low				High
	1	2	3	4	5
Will satisfy most of them	55%	74%	74%	82%	80%
Will satisfy some of them	33	22	23	15	20
Will satisfy a few of them	6	4	3	2	-
Will satisfy none of them	1	-	-	-	-
N	(132)	(489)	(592)	(272)	(86)

   Similarly, the self-confident men are the most optimistic
about their economic futures. When asked how much money
they expected to earn ten years after college graduation,[6]
56 percent of them expected to earn over $10,000 compared
with 32 percent of the least secure men. On the other hand,
25 percent of the former, compared with 44 percent of the
latter, expected to be earning under $7,500.

Table 18
Self-Confidence and Earnings Expectations (Men)

Earnings Expected in Ten Years	Self-Confidence				
	Low 1	2	3	4	High 5
Under $7,500	44%	34%	32%	27%	25%
$7,500-$10,000	25	30	23	23	19
Over $10,000	32	36	45	50	56
N	(85)	(307)	(426)	(188)	(64)

   These findings suggest that the anxious or insecure person
tends to be relatively discouraged about his career before he
starts. He is less likely to think that his work will really
give him what he wants out of it and he is less likely to
feel that he will make much money at his job.
   While it is not immediately clear how self-confidence
would influence occupational choice, one empirical finding
affords a suggestive hint. At one point in our study, respondents were presented with a list of six characteristics
and were asked to check the two characteristics most essential for success in the fields they had chosen. One of the
qualities on this list was "organizing and administrative
ability." Our data show that students expecting to enter the
fields of hotel management, business, sales-promotion, farming, government work, and personnel work, are the most likely
to feel that "organizing and administrative ability" are very
essential for success in their work. We will call these six
occupations the "organizing-administrative" fields.
   The interesting finding which emerges is that 46 percent
of the most self-confident people chose one of the "organizing-administrative" occupations, but that this was true of
only 20 percent of the most anxious people. In addition, as
we would expect, the self-confident person is most likely to
believe he possesses this ability (Table 20).
   Why should this be so? Although we lack data to check our
interpretation, our hypothesis would be that a person who
chooses an occupation requiring organizing and administrative

ability, such as hotel management, business, sales-promotion, running a farm, is one who is willing to *assume responsibility* for his actions. He is willing to make decisions and face the consequences of his actions, is willing to "take charge" when things have to be done, is willing to assume control of things and people. If this is so, then it is understandable that a person who is basically self-confident would be quite willing to enter such occupations.[7] But more

Table 19
*Self-Confidence and Selection
of "Organizing-Administrative" Occupations (Men)

Occupational Choice	Self-Confidence				
	Low				High
	1	2	3	4	5
Select "organizing-administrative" occupation	20%	26%	29%	34%	46%
Do not select "organizing-administrative" occupation	80	74	71	66	54
N	(91)	(332)	(445)	(203)	(70)

* Selected overwhelmingly by men.

important, probably, would be the tendency for the anxious or insecure person—the individual who is constantly worried, highly vulnerable to criticism, and lacking in self-confidence—to *avoid* an occupation in which he would have to take charge, make decisions, and assume responsibility for his actions. Although there is undoubtedly a wide personality range in every field, these data suggest that there is a selective recruitment of personality types to various occupations which may result in the emergence of different "modal personalities" in various fields.

Table 20
Self-Confidence and Belief that One Possesses
Organizing and Administrative Ability (Men)

"Organizing and administrative ability"	Self-Confidence				
	Low				High
	1	2	3	4	5
Believe they have it	40%	39%	55%	59%	68%
Do not believe they have it	60	61	45	41	32
N	(93)	(333)	(456)	(204)	(70)

"Self-Other" Attitudes

One aspect of personality which has received increasing attention in recent years is the concept of "self-other" attitudes[8]—attitudes which influence the individual's characteristic way of relating to other people. There is reason to believe that the way an individual relates to others will be reflected in his selection of those values he hopes to satisfy in his work and in his occupational choice. This is not to say that personality "causes" values; rather, our argument is that the selection of certain occupational values is partly an *expression* of certain personality characteristics which are not themselves values. An illustration of the type of finding we would anticipate on the basis of this hypothesis would be the following: if an individual tends to have a strong need for affective ties to others, if he is strongly oriented toward obtaining warmth and affection, then he will particularly value the opportunity to *work with other people* in his occupational practice. In other words, his basic interpersonal attitude *will find expression* in the gratification he seeks from work.

As Horney has observed in her works, there are three basic ways in which an individual may relate himself to others: he may "move toward," "move against," or "move away from" people.[9] Actually, it will be noted, this typology includes two dimensions. The first might be called the "domination-submission" dimension. At the submission end of the scale we would find the "moving toward" type, at the domination end of the scale the "moving against" type. The "moving away from" type cannot be classified on this dimension at all; he is ranged on the dimension of "distance from others." The "moving away from" type seeks to maintain distance between himself and people; the "moving toward" and "moving against" types seek to be *near* others, the latter in order to dominate them, the former in order to submit to them. The "moving away from" type neither wishes to dominate nor to submit.

To simplify our notation, we will use Horney's terms to characterize these types. Those who seek to "move toward people" are known as "the compliant type"; those who seek to "move against people" are called "the aggressive type"; and those who seek to "move away from people" are referred to as "the detached type."[10] These three types may be ranked along the above-mentioned dimensions in the following way:

Dimensions of Relationships to Others

Distance from Others	Domination-Submission		
	Dominant	Neutral	Submissive
	+	0	−
Near +	A (Aggressive)	B	C (Compliant)
Far −	D	E (Detached)	F

It will be noted that people in cells B, D, and F are not classified. Cells D and F are logically unlikely types, since it would be difficult to have as little to do with people as possible and still seek to either dominate them or submit to them. Cell B would come closest to a "healthy democratic personality"—a type who establishes close relationships with others but neither seeks to dominate nor to submit to them.

Since adequate data were not available in our study to enable us to differentiate these types in a sophisticated fashion, it was necessary to use various indirect questions in an effort to classify respondents crudely in terms of "pure" types.

The detached personality type has been characterized as one who desires to maintain his emotional distance from others; he tends to be deeply concerned with his independence and the expression of his individuality. Fundamentally resistant to coercion or domination of any sort, he chiefly wants no interference from the world.[11] In our study, we characterized people as detached if they said they were concerned with being "independent" (rather than "successful" or "well-liked"), said they were bothered at being given orders by others, considered it relatively unimportant for them to be well liked by different kinds of people, and said that, when in a group, they preferred to make decisions themselves rather than having others make the decisions.

The compliant type, on the other hand, is particularly concerned with approval, acceptance, warmth, support. He "likes everyone," is anxious to please them, is willing to be dominated but is reluctant to dominate others. We have classified people in this category if they said they were anxious to be "well liked," were not bothered by being given orders but were bothered at giving them, and expressed a positive view of human nature.

The aggressive type, finally, is concerned with mastery, control, domination and conquest in the external world. This

person is anxious to be top dog in a dog-eat-dog world; he
respects only the powerful and successful. Respondents have
been classified as belonging to this type if they were chiefly concerned with being "successful," (rather than independent
or well liked), if they said they did not mind giving orders
to other people, and if they said that "if you don't watch
yourself, people will take advantage of you."

Although the indices employed are undeniably crude, they
represent an attempt to differentiate people roughly in terms
of their major "self-other" orientations. The question now
becomes: what influence does this aspect of personality have
on occupational values and occupational choices?

The Self-Other Typology and Occupational Values

If our indices have successfully differentiated people in
terms of self-other orientations, then we would expect the detached people to be more likely than others to stress "freedom
from supervision" and "the chance to be creative and original"
as occupational values. The detached type is, in the first
place, characterized by a deep-seated resistance to coercion
or domination of any sort. The fact that 66 percent of the
detached people ranked "leave me relatively free of supervision" high as an occupational value, compared with 36 percent
of the others, suggests that a person who is predisposed to
emphasize independence in a variety of life situations will,
when asked about his occupational values, stress the notion of
freedom from control in this area as well.

Table 21
Detached Type and Occupational Values

	Detached Type	All Others
"Leave me free of supervision"		
Ranked high	66%	36%
Ranked low	7	14
"Permit me to be creative and original"		
Ranked high	68%	46%
Ranked low	8	13
Either "freedom" or "creative"		
Ranked high	84%	63%
Ranked low	14	24
N	(146)	(982)

Similarly, the fact that the detached person is so highly conscious of his unique individuality would help to account for his tendency to emphasize creativity and self-expression in his work (Table 21). It is this desire to be unique, different, and special which represents one of the strongest appeals of detachment, and it is understandable that this desire should tend to be reflected in occupational values.

When we turn to the *aggressive* personality type, a different occupational value constellation greets us—the "extrinsic-reward" values. The aggressive type is concerned with domination and mastery; it is well known that one very fertile area for the manifestation of such dominance in American society is the occupational field. Two ways of pushing ahead in the world and thereby establishing one's superiority over others are to earn "a good deal of money" and to gain a high degree of "status and prestige." It is these values, it turns out, that the aggressive people are particularly apt to select. As Table 22 indicates, nearly three-fourths of the aggressive people ranked one of these values highly important, compared with less than two-fifths of the remainder of the respondents. The general desire for success and mastery appears to be expressed specifically in the occupational area in the form of a desire for prestige and possession.

Table 22
Aggressive Type and Occupational Values

	Aggressive Type	All Others
"Earn a good deal of money"		
Ranked high	61%	31%
Ranked low	2	14
"Give me social status and prestige"		
Ranked high	44%	20%
Ranked low	9	22
Either "money" or "status"		
Ranked high	73%	39%
Ranked low	10	30
N	(186)	(942)

Finally, the *compliant* type—the type who wants to be liked, accepted, welcomed, who wants to do things for others—tends to project his personality into the occupational realm by stressing "people-oriented" values. He tends to stress that an ideal job must enable him to "work with people rather than things" and must give him an "opportunity to be helpful to others" (Table 23). This individual, anxious to please and be helpful, seeks a work experience which will enable him to do so.

Table 23
Compliant Type and Occupational Values

	Compliant Type	All Others
"Opportunity to work with people"		
Ranked high	53%	33%
Ranked low	14	28
"Opportunity to be helpful to others"		
Ranked high	45%	31%
Ranked low	14	21
Either "people" or "helpful"		
Ranked high	74%	48%
Ranked low	22	38
N	(96)	(1032)

It would appear, then, that if we are able to isolate relatively "pure" personality types, we find that these personality characteristics tend to be expressed in the selection of occupational values. In what sense is it meaningful, then, to speak of "values" and "personality" as separate concepts? Essentially, all we mean by the aspect of personality discussed here is some predisposition to behave in a certain fashion in a large number of situations. Values, too, are criteria which determine behavior, but which are socially defined as good or bad. Among the various things which the society encourages the individual to want (or not want), he will tend to select those which most closely agree with his underlying orientation. In this sense, occupational values would be a reflection of personality.

Self-Other Orientation and Occupational Choice

Every occupation has some interpersonal quality about it—the chance to enjoy interaction with other people, or to dominate them, or to get away from them; and, as we will show later, the students are keenly aware of the importance of interpersonal factors in their careers. In principle, then, the individual's self-other orientation might well have some bearing on his occupational choice. However, it is actually rather difficult to pin down this influence, since the same

occupation potentially can satisfy so many different values
for different people. Thus, personality alone can rarely determine a *specific* choice, although it may represent a channeling factor determining one's broad *area* of choices.

In general, we would expect that if a student selects
those values which are congenial to his "self-other orientation," he would also tend to choose an occupation in which,
it is generally believed, these values can be satisfied.

Take, for example, the compliant personality type. This
person, who wants to be well liked and to establish friendly
relations with other people, tends to select "people-oriented" values. We would thus expect him to be more likely than
others to select those occupations in which these values
could be fulfilled. As we observed in Chapter II, students
entering the fields of social work, medicine, teaching, social science, and personnel work were most likely to hold
people-oriented values. It turns out that 43 percent of the
compliant people chose one of these occupations, compared
with 24 percent of the students classified as detached or aggressive.

Similarly, it was observed that people entering the fields
of real estate or finance, hotel management, sales-promotion,
law, advertising, and business (unspecified) tended to emphasize the extrinsic rewards of work. These are the values
stressed by the aggressive personality type. Our data show
that 32 percent of those classified as aggressive chose one
of these fields, compared with 20 percent of the detached and
compliant people.

The detached personality type, finally, would be expected
to choose an occupation in which he felt the values of freedom from supervision and creativity and originality could be
realized. Students selecting the fields of art, architecture,
journalism-drama, and natural science tended to place the
greatest stress on these values. It turns out that 30 percent
of those classified as detached selected one of these fields,
compared with 14 percent of the aggressive and compliant
people (Table 24).

An additional item of evidence is available to suggest
that the detached person tends to select an occupation which
is consonant with his personality needs. We have noted that
the detached person tends to value his independence and freedom and dislikes anything hinting at regimentation or coercion; consequently, when he chooses a type of "firm or outfit"
in which he would like to work, we would expect him to select
one which would grant him *independence of action* and to avoid
the pressures of regularity and hierarchical discipline of a

large-scale organization. It is interesting to note, therefore, that when the respondents were asked what type of "firm
or outfit" they would like to enter, only 15 percent of the
detached people chose the category "private firm, organization, or factory, " compared with 36 percent of the other
people in the study. Thus the selection of a certain type of
organization appears to be associated with a desire to maintain an emotional distance between oneself and other people.

Table 24
Personality Typology and Choice of Occupational Area

Occupational choice:		Detached and
Social work, medicine, teaching, social science, and personnel	Compliant 43% (185)	Aggressive 24% (314)
Real estate, hotel, sales, law, advertising, & business (unspec.)	Aggressive 32% (188)	Detached and Compliant 20% (311)
Art, architecture, journalism-drama, and natural science	Detached 30% (126)	Compliant and Aggressive 14% (373)

Although the crudeness of our indices prevents us from
making any final judgments on the subject, the results appear
sufficiently suggestive to indicate that the way a person
characteristically relates to others will influence the type
of career he selects. In principle, it does seem to make
good sense to assume that an individual who "moves toward
people," wants to be loving and helpful, will be guided toward
a general area of occupations in which friendly, frequent
contact with others is inherent in the structure of the occupation. Similarly, a person who needs to express control,
mastery, or domination will move toward that general area of
occupations in which this desire can find expression. Finally, an individual who wants to have as little as possible to
do with others, wishes to maintain his emotional distance
from people, would tend to avoid occupations in which others
are likely to make demands upon him. In other words, if the
individual relates to others in a characteristic way in a
variety of life situations, it would not be surprising to
find that this type of relationship influences his occupational values and occupational choice.

CHAPTER V

SOCIAL DETERMINANTS OF OCCUPATIONAL CHOICES AND VALUES

Sex Status and Occupational Choice

In the college community no factor is so important for one's occupational future as socially defined sex roles. In almost every aspect of occupational values and choices, men and women tend to differ radically. To a minor extent these differences are explicable in terms of the physical requirements of the occupation—e. g., farming—but to an overwhelming extent, in the middle-class white-collar occupations chiefly selected by college students, it is entirely a question of how American society defines the place of men and women in the occupational structure.

In the first place, career plays a more important part in the total life plans of men. Table 25 shows that three times as many men expected their careers to represent their "major

Table 25
Expected Major Life Satisfactions of Men and Women

"What three things or activities in your life do you expect will give you the most satisfaction?"	Major Life Satisfactions			
	First Choice		Second Choice	
	Men	Women	Men	Women
Your career or occupation	25%	8%	52%	40%
Family relationships	62	83	26	12
Leisure-time recreational activities	6	2	12	25
Religious beliefs or activities	3	6	5	13
Participation as citizen in affairs of your community	1	1	3	12
Participation in activities directed toward national or international betterment	1	1	2	3
N	(2007)	(749)	(2007)	(749)

life satisfaction" as did women. In American society, men
expect to spend the major part of their lives at work; the
woman's long-range view tends to focus on family relationships. Whereas virtually none (less than one-half of one
percent) of the men did not expect to be working ten years
after graduation, this expectation was expressed by 52 percent of the women.

Not only does career occupy a different place in the total
life frameworks of men and women, but the values they hope
to satisfy at work are clearly at variance. Relatively
speaking, the women are people-oriented, the men extrinsic
reward-oriented. These data suggest that society, through
the inculcation of role prescriptions, encourages men and
women to want different things from their work (Table 26).
Although there has been a good deal of pressure in recent
years to bring about sexual equality of opportunity, differences in occupational "wants" are still strong.

Table 26
Occupational Values of Men and Women

Values	Most Important		Highly Important	
	Men	Women	Men	Women
Special abilities or aptitudes	28%	27%	78%	80%
Earn a good deal of money	9	3	36	19
Creative and original	10	10	49	54
Social status and prestige	2	1	25	15
Work with people rather than things	7	23	39	59
Stable, secure future	26	15	63	51
Free of supervision by others	6	3	46	40
Exercise leadership	2	1	38	29
Adventure	1	2	14	17
Opportunity to help others	6	13	37	53
N	(2008)	(750)	(2008)	(750)

But what about the "career-woman"—the girl who rejects
her sisters' overwhelming emphasis on family relationships
and looks to her occupational efforts as her major source of
life satisfaction? Has she also abandoned the characteristically female occupational values and shifted toward wanting
the same things out of work as men? (Table 27)

Table 27
Career-Orientation and Occupational Values
among Men and Women

Occupational Values	Major Life Satisfactions			
	Career First Choice		Career Low Choice	
Ranked Highly Important	Men	Women	Men	Women
Earn a good deal of money	30%	27%	43%	17%
Status and prestige	24	25	26	19
Work with people	38	39	39	69
Helpful to others	39	43	41	62
Creative and original	60	63	44	49
N	(492)	(56)	(503)	(404)

It may be noted that the occupational values of the career woman are almost identical with those of the career-oriented man. Among the noncareer-oriented people, however, men are clearly more concerned with extrinsic regards, women with working with people. In other words, sex roles are factors of importance in determining occupational values but not among women who have adopted a "male" attitude toward their occupations. The career woman tends to want to satisfy the values which men choose in work rather than the values selected by other women.

A fairly clear-cut sexual division of labor appears when we ask students what fields they expect to enter. Some fields are predominantly "women's occupations," others are overwhelmingly "men's occupations." (Table 28)

In our sample, half of the men desired to enter either law, engineering, farming, or business, but only one-twentieth of the women chose one of these occupations. Conversely, half of the women selected teaching, social work, secretarial work, art, or journalism-drama, compared with one-seventh of the men. Men and women thus tend to select distinctly different occupations.

Further evidence of the sexual division of labor appears when we ask students what type of organization they expect to work in. Women are much more likely than men to choose a humanitarian, educational, non-profit organization (Table 29). Compared with the male students, only a small minority of women expect to achieve occupational independence, in the sense of becoming independent entrepreneurs or professionals. Almost all of them will be subject to some sort of occupational supervision or domination.

In considering how men and women differ in their occupational values and choices, it may be noted that these results appear to have certain implications for the institutions of marriage and the family. On the most obvious level, for example, the finding that women show less emotional involvement in their careers, that only very rarely do they consider it their main probable source of life satisfaction, reduces the

Table 28
Occupational Choices of Men and Women

Occupation	Percent Choosing Each Occupation	
	Men	Women
Architecture	4	3
Engineering	24	1
Law	5	-
Medicine-Nursing	8	5
Teaching	10	35
Social work	1	5
Government work	2	2
Journalism-drama	2	4
Art	-	3
Hotel-Restaurant-Dietetics	6	10
Sales-promotion	6	4
Advertising-Public Relations	1	1
Personnel	4	2
Farming	13	2
Secretarial	1	4
Natural science	5	5
Social science	2	4
Business (unspecified)	6	2
Housewife	-	6
Real estate-Finance	1	-
N	(1649)	(599)

potential competition with their interest in family relationships. It is evident that where a woman has the greatest involvement and investment in a certain area of work, the well-known conflict between marriage and career is certain to be strongest. The fact that women are less encouraged to see their careers as a long-term or permanent focus of interest and satisfaction enables them to be more interested in marriage and less dissatisfied than they otherwise might be in performing the wife-mother role.

When we turn to the men's occupational values, we may note that they are more likely than women to place strong stress on the extrinsic rewards of work—money and security—rather than on the satisfactions inherent in the work relationship.

The usefulness of this value-orientation for the stability
of the family structure is obvious; such values increase the
man's reliability as a provider. In other words, the less
the man emphasizes whim, spontaneity, creativity, mood in
his work, and the more he emphasizes money and security, the
more stable is the family structure likely to be. There is
less shift in the functions performed by each family member,
patterns of expectations are clearer, and swift changes in
style of life which threaten family stability are fewer.
From the viewpoint of the family, then, men place *relatively*
high stress on those values most useful to them as family
providers.

Table 29
Type of Occupational Organization Selected
by Men and Women

Type of Firm or Outfit Desired	Men	Women
Own business or own farm	15%	3%
Own professional office	10	3
Educational institution	9	30
Social agency	2	8
Other non-profit organization	3	5
Government bureau or agency	8	5
Family business or enterprise	6	3
Private firm, organization, or factory	43	30
Other	3	4
Do not expect to work	1	9
N	(2007)	(749)

The third point to be noted is that men and women tend to
choose different occupations—there are "men's fields" and
"women's fields." The effect of this is to reduce *occupational competition* between the sexes. Such competition could
potentially pose a threat to the institution of marriage, for
if men and women wanted the same things out of work, went into the same occupations to get them, struggled for socially
scarce resources, and if this competition were of a long-term
and emotionally involved sort, the mutual antagonisms devel-
oping between the sexes might have serious implications for
the social norm of *romantic love*. And our data[1] agree with
the well-known fact that this is the chief criterion in the
decision to marry in American culture.
    Finally, it may be noted that women's occupational values
and choices are not irrelevant to their ultimate family
roles. Their strong emphasis on teaching at the lower educa-

tional level, involving the socialization of children, is too
obvious in its implications to require comment; and their emphasis on people-oriented values may not be irrelevant to
their ultimate family roles.

These observations suggest that if we are to understand
the occupational values and choices of young people in American society, particularly the values and choices of women, it
is necessary to consider the probable influence of "marriage
and the family" factors on their occupational orientations.

Family Economic Position

One of the fundamental elements of the American Creed is
that every man should have an equal opportunity to climb to
the top of the economic ladder, irrespective of his background. Neither family position nor any other ascribed
characteristic is supposed to be the basis for ultimate position in the society; rather, concrete occupational achievements, expressive of merit and industry, are presumed to be
the ultimate determinants. This formal doctrine manages to
hang on in the culture despite cumulative evidence indicating
the importance of family background in determining one's occupational level.

Generally speaking, we might expect family background to
be less important as a determinant of occupational expectations among college students than among young people in the
non-campus community. Only rarely are very poor people able
to go through college, and if they do they are likely to be
unusually anxious to get ahead in life. Nevertheless, our
data indicate that there is a definite relationship between
the amount of money the father currently earns and the amount
the student expects to earn in the future. At the extremes,
half of the poorest students expected to be earning no more
than $7,500 ten years after graduation, compared with one-
twentieth of the wealthiest respondents; conversely, nearly
nine-tenths of the latter group expected to exceed $10,000,
but only one-third of the former group (Table 30). Family
economic background is clearly a very important determinant
of expectations regarding one's own ultimate economic position.

Since the possibility of earning a good deal of money var-
ies from occupation to occupation, we would naturally assume
that students from higher economic backgrounds would tend to
select occupations which are known to have many wealthy practitioners. Business and the independent professions are

probably the most fruitful fields for the man who seeks to
make a good deal of money. It is therefore to be expected
that the higher one's family background, the more likely
would one be to choose these occupations. This is shown to
be the case in Table 31. Seventy-one percent of the wealthiest students planned to enter some branch of business or law
or medicine, compared with only 38 percent of the poorest
students. On the other hand, the less well-to-do student
tends to gravitate toward such salaried professions as engineering, teaching, social work, and science. This is understandable, since these occupations do not require the capital,
credit, or connections often essential for business success
nor do they involve graduate work as expensive as that required by the free professions of medicine and law.

Table 30
Father's Income by Student's Future Earnings Expectations

Student's Ex-pected Earnings In Ten Years	Father's Income						
	Under 3,000	3,000 5,000	5,000 7,500	7,500 10,000	10,000 20,000	20,000 30,000	Over 30,000
Under $7,500	50%	39%	39%	26%	14%	10%	5%
7,500-10,000	16	22	19	23	20	12	7
10,000-20,000	29	33	34	42	52	50	45
Over $20,000	5	6	7	9	13	28	43
N	(245)	(731)	(556)	(380)	(385)	(145)	(148)

It would thus appear that the objective fact of monetary
possession operates to channel the direction of occupational
choice. Recent developments in reference group theory,[2] however, compel us to consider whether the subjective factor of
social class identification may also be related to occupational choice. And we find, in fact, that whereas 66 percent
of the students who considered themselves members of the upper class selected either business or one of the independent
professions, this was true of only 48 percent of those iden-
tifying with the middle class, and 34 percent of the respondents who considered themselves in the working class. Conversely, nearly half the students considering themselves
working class selected one of the salaried professions of engineering, teaching, social work, or science, compared with
about one-third of the middle class members and one-sixth of
the upper class.
    Since both father's income and class identification are
related to the selection of similar occupations, and since
these two factors are strongly related to each other, it is

important to ask whether the objective fact of money and influence is crucial or whether people who *think* they are in
certain classes select occupations appropriate to their assumed statuses, irrespective of their families' incomes.

Table 31
Father's Income and Occupational Choice

Occupational Choice	Father's Income				
	Under $7,500	7,500 10,000	10,000 20,000	20,000 30,000	Over 30,000
Business and the free professions:					
Business (unspecified)	12	9	18	11	22
Real estate-Finance	1	3	4	6	7
Sales-promotion	4	2	6	7	3
Advertising-Publ. Reltns.	1	2	3	1	3
Hotel management	1	1	1	2	2
Law	5	9	9	13	16
Medicine	14	16	15	20	18
Total percent:	38	42	56	68	71
Some salaried professions:					
Engineering	19	15	14	13	10
Teaching	14	6	6	1	4
Social work	2	2	-	1	-
Science	10	9	6	6	2
Total percent:	45	32	26	21	16
Other occupations: *					
Total percent:	17	26	18	11	13
N	(1367)	(324)	(336)	(135)	(137)

* Includes architecture, art, journalism-drama, farming,
government work, and personnel work.

The results in Table 32 indicate that the objective factor
of family income is more important than subjective class identification in determining occupational choice. Among those
whose fathers earned under $10,000, there is a somewhat great-
er tendency for upper and middle class respondents to choose
"business" occupations, medicine, or law than working class
students, but these differences are considerably smaller than
those which appear when father's income is not considered
(Table 32). Among the rather wealthy students (those whose
fathers earned over $10,000 annually), the influence of class
identification upon occupational choice appears very weak.

Table 32

Class Identification and Occupational Choice by Father's Income

Occupational Choice	Under 5,000			5,000-7,500			7,500-10,000			10,000-20,000			20,000-30,000			Over 30,000		
	Up-per	Mid-dle	Work-ing	Up-per	Mid-dle	Work-ing	Up-per	Mid-dle	Work-ing	Up-per	Mid-dle	Work-ing	Up-per	Mid-dle	Work-ing	Up-per	Mid-dle	Work-ing
Business and the free professions**	-*	42	32	38	41	38	53	53	37	63	56	-	69	67	-	71	71	-
Some salaried professions***	-	41	50	29	42	46	19	31	31	15	30	-	17	23	-	12	20	-
N	(9)	(419)	(412)	(21)	(421)	(69)	(30)	(273)	(16)	(81)	(252)	(-)	(67)	(68)	(-)	(87)	(47)	(-)

* Groups containing fewer than ten cases are omitted
** Business, real estate, sales, advertising, hotel, medicine, law
*** Engineering, teaching, social work, science

On the other hand, it is clear that as family wealth increases, the tendency to choose "business" occupations, medicine, or law increases as well, even among those who identify
with the same social classes. The chief exception to this
generalization appears among those students who consider
themselves members of the working class; it is difficult to
interpret this finding, since so few wealthy students make
this identification. The general pattern, however, indicates
that objective economic position is more important than subjective class identification in determining these students'
occupational choices.

Table 33
Social Class Identification and Occupational Choice

Occupational Choice	Upper Class	Middle Class	Working Class
Business and the free professions: Business, real estate, sales-promotion, hotel, advertising, law, medicine	66%	48%	34%
Some salaried professions: Engineering, teaching, social work, science	17	35	48
Other occupations:	17	17	18
N	(342)	(1709)	(584)

Family economic background is thus far from irrelevant for
one's economic fate. For example, the finding that 66 percent
of the poorest students expected to earn under $10,000 com-
pared with only 12 percent of the wealthiest would point to
some inheritance of occupational level (if these expectations
are accurate). This finding is in agreement with other studies[3] on the subject. It is characteristic to interpret such
differences as indicative of *inequality of opportunity*, of
what Davis has called "fluid ascription."[4] The sons of
wealthy fathers have advantages all along the line; they receive the best early training, go to the outstanding colleges,
and go on for professional training (if necessary); when they
go to work, they can either enter flourishing businesses owned
by their fathers, or they can enter large organizations in
which their fathers are on the managerial level, or their families have contacts which make coveted jobs available to them,
or they have family capital or credit to engage in their own
ventures, and so on. Thus, although they may have to work
hard to achieve their ultimate lofty economic positions, their

paths are smoothed considerably by virtue of the fact that
they happened to be born into rich families.

However, it is important to consider the factor of *motiva-*
tion as well as opportunity as a determinant of future earnings expectations. Not only are more of the wealthy students
likely to have the chance to earn a good deal of money, but
(as Table 34 indicates) more of them are likely to have the
desire as well. For example, 53 percent of the students
whose fathers earned over $20,000 said that "the chance to
earn a good deal of money" was a "highly important" value to
them, compared with 34 percent of those whose family incomes
were under $7,500. Similarly, the wealthier students were
more likely than the poorer students to stress "status and
prestige" as an occupational value.

Table 34
Father's Income and Respondent's Occupational Values

Occupational Values Ranked Highly Important	Father's Income			
	Under 7,500	7,500- 10,000	10,000- 20,000	Over 20,000
Earn a good deal of money	34%	35%	39%	53%
Social status and prestige	23	27	31	34
N	(841)	(245)	(286)	(156)

Table 35 indicates that both father's income (which may
serve as a crude index of "opportunity") and the view that
"the chance to earn a good deal of money" is a highly important occupational value (which may serve as a crude index of
"motivation") are independently related to the student's
earnings expectations.

Table 35
Money as an Occupational Value and Earnings Expectations,
by Father's Income

Earnings Expectations	Father's Income							
	Under 7,500		7,500- 10,000		10,000- 20,000		Over 20,000	
	Importance of Money as Occupational Value							
	High	Med., Low	High	Med., Low	High	Med., Low	High	Med., Low
Under $5,000	19%	32%	9%	19%	5%	9%	4%	12%
5,000-7,500	44	42	36	44	29	41	13	15
7,500-10,000	19	13	28	16	25	28	15	18
Over $10,000	19	13	27	21	43	23	67	56
N	(275)	(530)	(80)	(145)	(108)	(163)	(78)	(68)

The finding that a larger proportion of wealthier students than poorer students considers the chance to earn a good deal of money and to gain status and prestige important occupational values is somewhat unexpected. It would have been reasonable to assume that precisely those people who lacked money and status would be more likely to insist upon the importance of these values in choosing an occupation. But apparently this is not so. Those who have a great deal of money want a great deal of money; those who have less want less. In any case, these data suggest the likelihood that the inheritance of economic level may be due not only to superior opportunity but also to the fact that more of the wealthier youngsters are imbued with the *value* of achieving a high income level.

Social Mobility

In which group is the *expectation* of getting ahead in life more prevalent—among the richer or the poorer students? On the basis of our discussion of the occupational value of earning a good deal of money, it would appear that the wealthier people are more likely to expect to be upwardly mobile. But such a conclusion would be too hasty, for it is first necessary to ask: what do we mean by "social mobility"?

In order to analyze this problem two points must be considered. The first is that there are different dimensions of mobility, different ladders one may seek to climb. One person may desire to acquire a good deal of *money*, whereas a second may be relatively unconcerned with money but may want to rise in the *prestige* hierarchy, and a third may be interested in acquiring *power* (but may be relatively indifferent to money and prestige). Many studies of social mobility fail to make explicit precisely what dimension is under consideration.

For the present, then, let us deal solely with economic expectations. Does the fact that more of the wealthier students expect to earn a good deal of money indicate that more of them expect to "get ahead" economically? When we consider this question in the light of empirical data, these data do not permit us to answer this question directly but, rather, force us to ask another: get ahead of what or whom? For it is evident that social mobility is a concept involving *relationships*; one goes up or down the stratification scale only with reference to some specified *base*.

In some cases, a person is considered upwardly mobile if he advances beyond the position attained by his family (intergenerational mobility). In other cases, however, the life line of the individual is the unit of analysis, and a person is said to be upwardly mobile if in his later years he has reached a higher position in life than in his earlier years (intra-generational mobility). Finally, a person may be considered upwardly mobile with reference to some general social standard; in this case, the individual is considered to have achieved success if he reaches a relatively high position in the society, irrespective of where he started.

Thus, when we ask students, "How do you expect your own future standard of living (economic income) to compare with that of the family in which you were brought up?" we find, as indicated in Table 36, that students from the poorer families tend to expect to exceed their families' standards of living whereas those from wealthier families do not. For the total group of students whose fathers earned over $10,000 a year, more actually expected a lower than a higher standard of living. Using the family as a base, and considering money as a mobility criterion, more of the poorer students expected to improve their economic statuses.

Table 36
Father's Annual Income and Expected Future Standard of Living
among Men

Own Expected Standard of Living Compared with That of Family	Father's Income					
	Under 3,000	3,000 5,000	5,000 7,500	7,500 10,000	10,000 20,000	Over 20,000
Higher	76%	60%	42%	25%	15%	14%
About the same	23	39	55	64	70	62
Lower	1	1	3	11	14	24
N	(156)	(363)	(315)	(244)	(271)	(155)

Thus the question, "Is the wealthy or the poor student more likely to expect to get ahead economically?" must be answered in the following way. If we mean by "get ahead economically" the expectation of surpassing one's family, then the poorer student has greater mobility expectations. But if we mean by "get ahead economically" the desire to acquire a great deal of money in terms of some absolute social standard, then the wealthier person appears to expect greater upward mobility. In fact, Table 37 indicates that the relationship between expecting to earn a great deal of money and expecting to have a standard of living (economic income) higher than one's parents is not very strong. These data highlight the importance for writers on social mobility to indicate clearly the dimension of mobility under consideration and to specify the base from which the presumed mobility occurs.

Table 37
Expected Future Standard of Living
and Future Earnings Expectations

Earnings Expected Ten Years After Graduation	Own Expected Standard of Living (Economic Income) Compared with That of Family		
	Higher	About the Same	Lower
Under $5,000	17%	22%	25%
5,000-7,500	38	38	39
7,500-10,000	20	18	17
Over $10,000	26	23	19
N	(615)	(803)	(110)

Aside from the methodological question of how empirical research compels us to separate and clarify the various elements of a theoretical concept, the central substantive point is that there is a clear-cut relationship between one's economic background and the place of money in the perception of one's career. Those students who have a good deal of money now tend more than others to want it in the future. The wealthier student is more likely than the poorer one to emphasize the importance of earning a good deal of money as a career value, to choose an occupation with the greatest possibilities for high earnings, and to expect to make more money in the future. Expressed in other terms, he has the opportunity, the desire, and the confidence. These conditions favor the fulfillment of his expectations.

CHAPTER VI

SYSTEMS OF OCCUPATIONAL CIRCULATION

Social life is a dynamic, ever-shifting, ever-moving proc-ess, and this is probably as true of the process of occupa-tional choice as of most other areas of social action. At first glance there is a sense of endless milling, shuffling, and shifting in seemingly random fashion among students until a final occupational choice is made. In our study, fully 60 percent of the people who wanted to enter a particular occu-pation in 1950 had changed their minds by 1952.[1] The ques-tion is whether any system, any order, can be detected in the circulation among fields.

In order to study the process of change through time in detail, it is important to study the *same* people as they move in and out of occupations. For if we simply examine the num-ber of people selecting a particular occupation at two points in time, it is easy to overlook the complex process of turn-over which may have occurred during the interim.

Take the profession of medicine, for example. In 1950, 52 members of our sample expected to become doctors whereas in 1952 there were 46 people with this intention. Looking only at these figures, one might be inclined to say that this 12 percent loss was probably attributable to people's recogni-tion of the reality factors involved in the study of medicine. However, it would certainly appear that the occupational choices over a period of two years showed a good deal of sta-bility. Analysis of the panel data indicates that this im-pression of stability is quite misleading. What we actually find is that of the 52 students who originally wanted to en-ter the field of medicine, two years later 24 of these people—fully 46 percent—had changed their minds and decided either to enter other professions or did not know what occupation they preferred. At the same time 18 people who had originally made other choices or no choices now wanted to become doctors. Otherwise expressed, at one time or another fully 70 people considered medicine as a profession—28 people choosing medi-cine both times, 24 people leaving medicine for some other

profession, and 18 people leaving some other profession to
enter medicine. With regard to medicine, one-and-one-half
times as many people changed as did not change. The picture
of stability of choice revealed by a mere 12 percent trend
drop is plainly distorted.

This type of result appears many times in our study. For
certain purposes, of course, such trend data may be completely adequate, e. g., if medical schools wanted to predict what
proportion of a certain body of underclassmen would, as up-
perclassmen, apply for entry into medical schools. If they
wanted to know how these students made up their minds and
how stable their choices had been, however, then the panel
(reinterview) method would be indispensable.

Stability and Lability of Occupational Choice

The young person in college is still groping his way
toward adulthood, is still forming a picture of the type of
person he would like to be in the future. It is rather to
be expected, therefore, that in the course of a fairly long
period of time—two years—he would show a rather high rate
of change of occupational choice; and this expectation is
borne out by the facts. Such change is particularly likely
because the student has had at most a very limited experience
in actual occupational practice. Since he is called upon to
decide in a situation in which his knowledge is meager and
the range of alternatives wide, it is probable that such decisions would tend to be tentative.

In what occupations are changes most likely to occur? In
order to develop an adequate picture of turnover within an
occupation, we have found it useful to construct an "index
of changeability," computed by dividing the number of people
either entering or leaving the occupation by the number originally entering the occupation. (Occupations with under 25
cases in 1950 are starred in Table 38.)

Is there any outstanding factor which appears to differentiate the stable from the changeable occupations? The most
conspicuous difference appears to be the length and intensity
of training required for occupational practice. *With the exception of social work,*[2] *none of the seven most changeable
occupations involved specialized and long-term training for
occupational practice.* Including starred occupations, these
included housewife, advertising-public relations, government
service, social work, business, journalism-drama-art, and
secretarial work. *Contrariwise, all of the seven least*

*changeable occupations require specialized professional
training.* These include engineering, hotel administration,
architecture, medicine, law, teaching, and farming.

Table 38
Occupations Ranked in Order of Size of Indices of Changeability

	Occupation	Index of Changeability
*1.	Housewife	3.44
*2.	Advertising-Public Relations	2.43
*3.	Government service	2.20
*4.	Social work	2.09
5.	Business, etc.	1.51
6.	Journalism-Drama-Art	1.31
*7.	Secretarial work	1.31
8.	Personnel	1.30
*9.	Social science	1.19
10.	Natural science	1.16
11.	Farming	1.00
12.	Teaching	.96
13.	Law	.83
14.	Medicine	.81
15.	Architecture	.77
16.	Hotel administration	.70
17.	Engineering	.51

In order to obtain a clearer idea of the meaning of these
results, it is necessary to understand the administrative
structure of Cornell University. The Cornell panel with
which we are dealing consists of undergraduate students in
seven colleges of the University, namely, Agriculture,
Architecture, Arts and Sciences, Engineering, Home Economics,
Hotel Administration, and Industrial and Labor Relations.
The three largest colleges at Cornell are Arts and Sciences,
Engineering, and Agriculture. In addition, the University
has a number of professional schools for students who have
graduated from college, including a Medical School in New
York City and a Law School in Ithaca. It also has a program
of teacher training leading to certification.

With the exception of the College of Arts and Sciences,
therefore, students entering any of the other colleges as un-
dergraduates begin to receive training in the fields of specialization of their respective colleges. It is in these
fields of specialization that the lowest degree of change occurs. Students in the colleges of Engineering, Home
Economics, Hotel Administration, and Architecture are the

most stable in their occupational choices.   These are followed by Medicine, Law, and Teaching.   It will be noted that
these latter fields require specialized training; in Law and
Medicine, however, students have not officially started such
training but are usually taking some courses in preparation
for such advanced work.   A somewhat higher degree of change
is found in the field of farming, for which specialized
training is obtained at the College of Agriculture.

In general, then, it appears possible to make the following statement: in those fields requiring extensive specialized training, in which this training is started at the undergraduate level, we find the smallest amount of occupational turnover; in those fields requiring specialized training,
in which the official formal training has not started at the
undergraduate level but in which some preparation may be under way, the amount of turnover is somewhat higher; and in
those fields requiring relatively little specialized training, the amount of turnover is highest.   Two exceptions to
this statement are the fields of "personnel," for which
training is obtained at the School of Industrial and Labor
Relations, and "social work," for which no specialized training is available at Cornell.

These data make it evident that *specialization* is an important factor in the ultimate crystallization of occupational choice.   In other words, if we take two freshmen, aged
eighteen, entering Cornell at the same time, one of whom
tells us he plans to be an engineer, the other claiming he
wants to be an artist, the likelihood of change of occupational choice—other things being equal—will be much smaller
in the case of the former than of the latter.

The psychological reasons for this assumption can probably
be accounted for in terms of a theory of *involvement and investment*.   Our expectation would be that people might feel
just as tentative in their selection of a stable as of a
changeable occupation at the outset.   However, as they begin
to take courses in their fields, even if these be pre-medical
or pre-law courses, they develop a certain involvement in the
problems and content of the field which tends to anchor their
choices.   This interest is probably reinforced by regular interaction with other people who are becoming technical spe-
cialists.

The cumulation of specialized courses not only enhances
involvement, but produces an investment in time and energy
which the individual may be reluctant to discard.   The young
man in his fourth year of engineering school who suddenly develops a strong interest in philosophy may feel the sense of

waste in changing fields more poignantly than someone who has
concentrated in the Humanities with a major in English Literature.   There is so much technical specialization which is
not transferable to other fields that the sense of waste involved in leaving a technical field is likely to be very
strong; hence, technical specialization may serve as a valuable early predictor of ultimate crystallization of choice.

The Flow toward Culturally Standard Occupations

    Does increased maturity bring with it an increased tenden-
cy to select certain apparently "prosaic" and "down-to-earth"
occupations?   If so, this would suggest an increasing awareness of certain reality factors in occupational choice.   In
order to examine this question, we have ranked occupations in
terms of the proportion of new entrants to original entrants
by dividing the number of people newly entering the occupation in 1952 by the number originally making this occupational choice in 1950.   (Occupations containing under 25 cases in
1950 are starred in Table 39).

Table 39
Occupations Ranked in Order of Proportion of New Entrants to Original Entrants

	Occupation	Proportion of New to Original Entrants
*1.	Housewife	2.67
*2.	Advertising-Public relations	1.71
*3.	Government service	1.33
*4.	Social work	1.18
5.	Business, etc.	.88
*6.	Secretarial	.54
7.	Natural science	.52
8.	Journalism-Drama-Art	.48
9.	Personnel	.43
*10.	Social science	.38
11.	Teaching	.38
12.	Law	.37
13.	Medicine	.35
14.	Farming	.31
15.	Food-Hotel	.30
16.	Engineering	.23
17.	Architecture	.12

Among the more frequently chosen occupations, "business" has the highest proportion of new recruits with a ratio of .88; among the less chosen occupations, "housewife" leads with a ratio of 2.67. In 1950, 83 people planned to enter the general area of business. By 1952, this number had risen to 104 people, representing an increase of 25 percent. In 1950, nine people said they expected to be housewives. Two years later, 26 girls made this choice, nearly three times the original number.

These data suggest that there may be some tendency for students, as they mature, to move toward the more customary (and probably prosaic) occupations of business and homemaking. Whether this involves a process of disenchantment with other more glamorous fields, a reluctant resignation to reality, or a positive embracing of new social roles, are questions requiring more intensive analysis. It seems likely in any case that certain pressures are operating to produce greater agreement between the aspirations of young people, on the one hand, and the needs of society, on the other.

Changes in Occupational Values

We might be inclined to assume that the shift toward business and homemaking would indicate a trend toward the abandonment of the more idealistic and high-minded occupational values in favor of the more prosaic extrinsic rewards. Such a trend, in fact, has been observed and deplored by Ginzberg and his associates in their qualitative studies of occupational choice. They note:

Among the younger group which we interviewed (11- to 15-year-olds), there was much preoccupation with finding 'interesting' work. These youngsters conceived of work as an important area which could yield important satisfactions. It was somewhat disturbing, therefore, to find in the upper age groups an increasingly 'instrumental' attitude toward work. Among the college group, the emphasis shifted from consideration of using one's capacities, satisfying one's interests, and making a constructive contribution to society to the returns that can be obtained from a job in the form of income, pleasant working conditions, prestige, etc. Some of the difficulties of occupational choice may indeed be rooted in the fact that, under the pressure of social value schemes, we are too much preoccupied with the returns from work and that we are little concerned with how to find pleasure from work.[3]

The data from the Cornell study suggest, however, that
Ginzberg's fears may be ill-founded, for not only does no
such trend appear but, in some cases, the opposite results
may be found. This is rather clearly illustrated in Table
40, in which we find a *decreasing* concern with the extrinsic
reward of security and an *unchanged* concern with money and
status. On the other hand, there is no decrease in concern
with the self-expressive value of using one's abilities and
aptitudes, and an *increase* in emphasis on being creative and
original.

Table 40
Occupational Values Rated Highly Important by the
Same Students in 1950 and 1952

Values	1950 (Freshmen, Sophomores)	1952 (Juniors, Seniors)
Extrinsic rewards:		
Security	63%	46%
Money	33	33
Status	21	22
Self-expression:		
Creative and original	46	51
Use abilities, aptitudes	79	79
N	(944)	(944)

Although we do not have panel data for the nation-wide
sample, it is significant to see that the higher one's college class, the less the concern with security and the greater the concern with using one's creative potentialities at
work. Interest in money and status differs only slightly
among people at different stages of college progress (Table
41).

Table 41
Occupational Values Rated Highly Important
by Members of Various College Classes (Nation-wide Sample)

Occupational Values Rated Highly Important	First	Year in College Second	Third	Fourth & Fifth
Creative and original	43%	45%	48%	53%
Use abilities, aptitudes	75	76	78	79
Security	69	63	58	53
Earn a good deal of money	41	39	37	37
Status and prestige	23	25	26	27
N	(1103)	(1040)	(1181)	(1251)

The consequences of this value change for society may be
considered from two viewpoints. On the one hand, the increasing tendency to view work as a goal value rather than
as an instrumental value represents a windfall for society.
It suggests that relatively highly qualified personnel may
be motivated to perform functional tasks at low social cost.
If the work is such that many people enjoy doing it, then
there will be strong competition for the job and society
will not have to offer other socially scarce rewards to have
the job well filled. In addition, the stress on self-expression in work means that people are more likely to apply their
creative potentialities to the task instead of simply doing
a perfunctory job.

On the other hand, it may be that many present-day large-
scale bureaucratic organizations operate best with people
who are motivated to do their jobs competently rather than
"creatively." In these cases there is likely to be restive-
ness, frustration, and disruption of the organizational operation. By and large, however, it is probable that the upper levels of the middle class occupations to which these
students aspire allow considerable room for creativity (at
least compared with other occupations), so that the value
shift toward self-expression in work is probably more satisfactory to the individual and useful for the economic structure.

Aspirations and Expectations

In a society which in principle sets no limits to the
dreams of young people, one might expect a good deal of conflict to develop as people become increasingly aware of the
toughness of reality. A young man's fondest dream may be to
become a concert pianist, but he may recognize with a feeling
of despondency that he lacks the requisite talent. He might
then resign himself to the prospect of working in his father's business. How widespread are conflicts of this sort?
Actually, as far as our data permit us to judge, it would appear that the conflict between what the student wants and
what he expects to get is not very strong in the first place,
and that in the course of time this *conflict grows progressively weaker*.

The students in our nation-wide sample were asked, "What
business or profession would you *most like* to go into? (Occupation or kind of work?)" and "What business or profession
do you realistically think you are most likely to go into (as

your life career)?" The answers to the first question reveal
that the sense of free choice is severely limited by reality
considerations. Our respondents do not say that they would
"most like" to be millionaire playboys and men-about-town or
industrial tycoons, although these answers might be true.
Rather, we find that most of the students "desire" to enter
those occupations they realistically expect to enter, and
these expectations usually are practical and feasible. In 78
percent of the cases, aspirations and expectations were identical; students wanted and expected to become engineers, doctors, lawyers, teachers, government workers, farmers, etc.

It should be remembered, of course, that we are dealing
with a special group—people who are probably well along on
the road toward their occupational objectives by the time
they are in college. Nevertheless, we would hypothesize that
this result is to some extent the product of an on-going
psychological process leading to the progressive reduction of
conflict.

One way of studying this process in detail is to examine
the mutual interaction of occupational aspirations and expectations at two separate points in time. Take, for example,
the relationship between desires and expectations in the
fields of medicine, business, and teaching in 1950 and 1952
(Tables 42, 43, and 44).

Table 42
Aspirations and Expectations of Becoming
Doctors in 1950 and 1952

1952	1950				
	Desire; Expect	Desire; Not Expect	Not Desire; Expect	Not Desire; Not Expect	Total
Desire-Expect	26	3	-	15	44
Desire-Not expect	4	3	-	2	9
Not desire-Expect	1	-	1	-	2
Not desire-Not expect	19	17	3	850	889
Total	50	23	4	867	944

In order to reduce awkwardness in discussion, we will refer to those who desired to enter a particular field and expected to do so as + + ; those who desired to enter the field
but did not expect to do so as + - ; those who did not desire,
but did expect, to enter a field as - + ; and those who
neither desired nor expected to enter a field as - - . What
pattern of change emerges from an examination of aspirations
and expectations in 1950 and 1952?

Table 43
Aspirations and Expectations of Becoming
Businessmen in 1950 and 1952

1952	1950				
	Desire; Expect	Desire; Not Expect	Not Desire; Expect	Not Desire; Not Expect	Total
Desire-Expect	13	4	3	46	66
Desire-Not expect	2	-	-	20	22
Not desire-Expect	1	-	1	14	16
Not desire-Not expect	11	23	39	767	840
Total	27	27	43	847	944

First, let us look at the field of medicine (Table 42).
Both in 1950 and 1952 there was a strong relationship between
desires and expectations; people who wanted to become doctors
tended to expect realistically that they would enter this
field, and those who did not want to become doctors did not
expect to enter it. However, it is important to note that
between 1950 and 1952 the number of people in conflict decreased. In 1950, there were 27 people in conflict (23 + -
and 4 - +), whereas in 1952 there were only 11 people in
conflict (9 + - and 2 - +).

Table 44
Aspirations and Expectations of Becoming
Teachers in 1950 and 1952

1952	1950				
	Desire; Expect	Desire; Not Expect	Not Desire; Expect	Not Desire; Not Expect	Total
Desire-Expect	39	3	6	30	78
Desire-Not expect	7	3	-	14	24
Not desire-Expect	1	2	4	10	17
Not desire-Not expect	34	19	27	745	825
Total	81	27	37	799	944

This reduction in the total amount of conflict was the result of a twofold process. Of the 27 people who originally
were in conflict in 1950, fully 23 of them had resolved this
conflict one way or the other by 1952; their aspirations and
expectations were now in harmony, as far as the field of medicine was concerned. However, of the 917 people who were
either + + or - - in 1950, seven of them had developed a con-

flict during the two-year span.   In the next section we will
consider in detail how these conflicts tended to be resolved.
For our present purposes, however, it is sufficient to note
that most of the inconsistent people resolved their conflicts
but a smaller number developed inconsistencies; hence, the
total amount of conflict for the group decreased.[4]

A similar pattern prevails when we examine the figures for
businessmen and teachers.   Take the businessmen (Table 43).
Here again the total number of people in conflict decreases.
In 1950, there were 70 people in conflict (27 + - and 43 - +),
whereas by 1952, only 48 were in conflict (22 + - and 16 - +).
Actually, of the 70 people who were originally in conflict in
1950, fully 69 had resolved this conflict two years later one
way or another.   However, a number of people who originally
had nothing to do with business now either wanted or expected
to enter the field, but not both.   Thus, while 69 out of 70
people were resolving their conflicts, 37 out of 874 were *de-
veloping* a conflict with regard to this field.

The teachers, finally, present a similar picture (Table
44).   On the first wave, 64 were inconsistent (27 + - and 37
- +), whereas on the second wave, 41 were in conflict (24 + -
and 17 - +).   As in the other two groups, most of the people
initially in conflict ultimately resolved it.   In this case,
55 of the 64 originally inconsistent people had achieved consistency two years later.   However, of the 880 people who
were originally consistent with regard to this field, 32 now
had aspirations and expectations which were dissonant.

We thus find that most people expect to go into the fields
they desire; those who are in conflict tend to resolve it one
way or the other; and a smaller number bring their conflicts
into the field.   It is possible that most people in this last
group, in turn, will eventually resolve their conflicts, only
to be replaced by a still smaller number who newly develop
conflicting aspirations and expectations with regard to the
occupation.

As far as these students are concerned, then, it would appear that the relationship between what one wants and what
one expects is initially quite close[5] and that in the course
of time it becomes closer.   Put in other terms, the general
movement appears to be in the direction of *average tension-
reduction*; there are fewer people in conflict on the second
wave than on the first.   In some cases the aspirations change,
in other cases, the expectations; either change has the effect of reducing potential frustration.

The consistency of these results suggests the possibility
that we may be witnessing the operation of some "law of circu-

lation" in the field of occupational choice. If so, it would underscore the importance of seeking uniformities of process in social science research as well as focusing on the relationships among static variables.

Mutual Interaction of Aspirations and Expectations

Since the discrepancy between what the student wanted and what he expected to get tended to decrease during the two-year span, it is interesting to investigate which factor—the desires or the expectations—was more important in bringing about the change. Did the student change his occupational desires to agree with his realistic expectations, or did he modify his view of the objective reality in such a way that he now expected to get what he wanted?

One method of studying which of two variables has the greater effect on the other was illustrated in the analysis of occupational values and choices (Chapter II). In the present problem, however, there are so few cases in many of the cells that the results are necessarily unreliable. However, it is still possible to study this mutual interaction by examining how people who are initially inconsistent ultimately resolve their conflicts. These data can be extracted from Tables 42, 43, and 44 by examining the + -'s and - +'s in 1950 who became either + + or - - in 1952. In order to show this change more clearly, we have put these data into new tables below (Tables 42A, 43A, and 44A).

Table 42A
Resolution of Conflict in the Field of Medicine
Between 1950 and 1952

1952	1950 Desire-Not Expect	Not Desire-Expect
Desire-Expect	3	—
Not desire-Not expect	17	3

When we look at the field of medicine, we find that of the 20 people who originally wanted to become doctors but did not expect to do so, 17 later on neither desired nor expected to enter this field. For these people, then, the expectations with regard to this field remained the same, but the aspirations changed to agree with them. On the other hand, in 6 cases the expectations changed to accord with the aspirations (3 + - people who became + + , and 3 - + people who became

- -). For the total group, however, more aspirations tended
to change to accord with expectations than the other way
around.

Table 43A
Resolution of Conflict in the Field of Business
Between 1950 and 1952

	1950	
1952	Desire-Not Expect	Not Desire-Expect
Desire-Expect	4	3
Not desire-Not expect	23	39

In the field of business, as Table 43A shows, the opposite
pattern prevails. In 43 cases, the expectations changed to
accord with the desires (4 + - who changed to + + and 39 - +
who changed to - -), whereas in 26 cases, the desires changed
to accord with the expectations (3 - + who changed to + + ,
and 23 + - who changed to - -). In this case, then, expectations tended to change in accord with aspirations.

Table 44A
Resolution of Conflict in the Field of Teaching
Between 1950 and 1952

	1950	
1952	Desire-Not Expect	Not Desire-Expect
Desire-Expect	3	6
Not desire-Not expect	19	27

Finally, among the teachers (Table 44A), aspirations and
expectations were nearly equal in mutual influence. In 30
cases, the desires remained the same and the expectations
changed to agree with them (3 + - who changed to + + , and
27 - + who changed to - -), and in 25 cases the desires
changed to agree with the expectations (6 + - who changed to
+ + , and 19 - + who changed to - -).

Thus, if we apply the concept of "relative importance"
loosely, we might say that in the field of medicine expectations are more important, in the field of business aspirations
are more important, and in the field of teaching both are
about equally important. What may account for these results?

The answer appears to lie in the "brittleness" or "soft-
ness" of the expectations. These, in turn, are related to
the permeability of the occupation, *i. e.*, the ease with
which one can enter or leave the field. For example, it is

relatively easy for a man who has been in college several years to decide one day that he no longer wants to be a history teacher but that he will go into business instead. It is less easy for him to decide to become a doctor. He may lack the money, his grades may be too low, he may have taken the wrong courses. In other words, there are fewer contingent reality factors involved in entering business; consequently, one's desires hold greater sway, with the expectations rather willing servants to these desires. On the other hand, all the hard willing in the world will not enable the youth with very low grades or the one who has not taken the appropriate preparatory courses to be accepted into medical school, and he knows it; consequently, the desires tend to fall into line with the more inexorable reality. The teacher is between the doctor and the businessman in this regard.

The same situation tends to hold true, though in lesser degree, with regard to leaving a field. It is not too difficult for a youth who has taken it for granted that he will enter his uncle's business to decide one day that he enjoys dramatics and will go on the stage. It is less easy for a medical aspirant to do this (and even less for an engineer or architect) who has committed himself to the extent of taking courses appropriate to this area and who has had time to develop some degree of involvement in the problems of medicine.

Thus we may say that where the permeability of a field is great, i. e., where it is relatively easy to enter or leave, the plans will tend to be the servant of desires; where permeability is limited, desires will go along with realistic expectations. This interpretation is supported by the data presented in Table 38. There an "index of changeability" was computed for each occupation, which was determined by dividing the number of people either entering or leaving the occupation at the time of the second wave by the number originally planning to enter the occupation in 1950. The index of changeability for the field of business was high—1.51, indicating that it was considered fairly easy to enter this field or drop out of it, whereas for the field of teaching it was .96, and for the field of medicine it was .81. The higher the index of changeability, the more the desires hold sway; the lower the index of changeability, the more the expectations are dominant. As we pointed out in an earlier section, those occupations in which students have already undertaken specialized training are the least changeable, whereas those occupations with little specialized training (and no involvement and investment) are the most changeable.

To repeat, there appears to be an element of flexibility in occupational desires which bends to the toughness of reality. If entry into the occupation is considered easy, then the aspirations hold sway; but if it is perceived as difficult, then the individual tends to modify his aspirations in terms of what he believes the external situation will enable him to get.

CHAPTER VII

CHANGE IN INDIVIDUAL CHOICES

Why does the student change his mind about his career? This question can be analyzed from two points of view. The first is illustrated by an earlier finding that students selecting occupations requiring the most intensive specialized training were least likely to change their occupational choices. In this finding, our analysis is focused on the characteristics of the *occupation* which promote or inhibit change of choice. But there is also a second question which may be raised, namely, what accounts for change or stability of occupational selection among *individuals* who have chosen the *same* occupation?

Since it is necessary to single out specific occupations for analysis, we have focused our attention on four fields. Three of these—engineering, business, and teaching—have been selected simply because they contain a relatively large number of cases; the fourth—medicine—while somewhat deficient in number of cases, has been chosen because it is the focus of a good deal of recent interest in the field of occupational sociology.[1] Engineering, unfortunately for our purposes, turns out to have relatively few changes, but the other occupational groups have very substantial proportions. In view of the relatively small N's with which we deal, we have applied standard measures of statistical significance to our results. However, it is virtually impossible to establish all the required controls because of the small number of cases and the appalling shrinkage. Adequate controls in most cases would produce wild, random fluctuations resulting from a variation of one or two cases. As a consequence, the results cited in this section are at best suggestive of the factors influencing change of occupational choice. We cannot be certain that in some cases spurious factors are not responsible for the relationships.

Values and Ideology

   Occupational values—We observed in Chapter II that people
planning to enter different occupations varied in the values
they hoped to satisfy in their work, and that the occupational choices and occupational values appeared to be, very broadly speaking, in "harmony." For example, social workers chose
"people-oriented" values; artists selected "self-expressive"
values; and businessmen stressed "extrinsic-reward" values.
However, what about those people who were in conflict, *i. e.*,
people who hoped to satisfy values other than those stressed
in their occupations? Our expectation would be that these
people would be more likely to change their occupational
choices than those whose occupations and values were in
"harmony."

   Let us first deal with the teachers in the panel. We
noted earlier that teachers were more likely than members of
most other occupational groups to choose "people-oriented"
occupational values. These values, it will be recalled, are
"give me an opportunity to work with people rather than
things" and "give me an opportunity to be helpful to others."
Our expectation would be that those teachers ranking one of
the "people-oriented" values high in importance in 1950 would
be less likely than others to abandon the field of teaching
in 1952.

Table 45
Occupational Values and Change of Occupational Choice
among Teachers*

People choosing teach- ing in 1950 who:	Occupational Values of Teachers, 1950	
	People-Oriented	Non-People-Oriented
Remained teachers, 1952	57%	19%
Left teaching, 1952	43	81
N	(82)	(26)

   * Percentage differences statistically significant at .01
level.

   The first point to note in Table 45 is that people desiring to enter teaching in 1950 characteristically ranked one
of the "people-oriented" values high; of the 108 teachers at
that time, 82 chose one or both of these occupational values
and 26 did not. More important, however, is the fact that of
those teachers who did select "people-oriented" values in
1950, 43 percent had left teaching two years later; but among

the teachers who did not hold these values, 81 percent had
changed their occupational choices. Put in other terms, members of the former group were exactly three times as likely
to *maintain* their occupational choices than were those in the
latter group. In the case of teachers, it is evident that if
people are not concerned with satisfying the occupational
values predominantly held in the occupation they have chosen,
they are more likely to desire a different occupation two
years later.

Now let us consider whether people who did *not* choose
teaching in 1950, but selected "people-oriented" values, were
more likely to *become* teachers in 1952 than were non-teachers
who did *not* select "people-oriented" values.

Table 46
"People-Oriented" Values and Choice of Teaching,
among Those Who Were Non-Teachers in 1950*

People who did not choose teaching in 1950 who:	Occupational Values, 1950 "People-Oriented"	"Non-People-Oriented"
Became teachers in 1952	7.5%	4.2%
Remained non-teachers in 1952	92.5	95.8
N	(451)	(385)

* Percentage differences statistically significant at .05
level.

Since so few non-teachers switched to teaching between
1950 and 1952, absolute differences are naturally small.
(For this reason, we have computed the percentages to one
place beyond the the decimal point.) Nevertheless, it turns
out that non-teachers holding "people-oriented" values are
significantly more likely to switch to teaching than non-
teachers who fail to hold these values.

Thus, the finding that teachers holding "people-oriented"
values were more likely to *remain* teachers than those who
held other values exclusively, and that non-teachers holding
"people-oriented" values were more likely to *become* teachers
than other non-teachers, points clearly to the influence of
occupational values on change or stability of occupational
choice.

Let us turn now to the occupational area of business. We
noted in Chapter II that one outstanding fact about the business group which broadly distinguishes it from the professional group is its concern with instrumental, "extrinsic-reward-
oriented" values. We get the clear-cut impression that, rel-

ative to the professional, the businessman is unconcerned with
self-fulfillment, helping others, or otherwise enjoying his
work. Rather, he is relatively more likely to insist that his
ideal job would have to "...provide me with a chance to earn a
good deal of money" and "give me social status and prestige."

Table 47
Occupational Values and Change of Occupational Choice among Businessmen*

People choosing business in 1950 who:	Occupational Values of Businessmen, 1950	
	Money-Status Values	Non-Money-Status Values
Remained businessmen, 1952	57%	32%
Left business, 1952	43	68
N	(42)	(37)

* Percentage differences statistically significant at .05
level.

Table 47 indicates that among businessmen, too, the tendency to hold the occupational values characteristic of the group
exercises an influence upon the decision to change one's occupational choice. Although there are many businessmen who do
not hold the "extrinsic-reward-oriented" values, businessmen
as a group are more likely to make this choice than are members of any other occupational group. It is thus interesting
to note that among the businessmen who selected these values
in 1950, 57 percent continued to choose business as their desired occupations two years later, compared with 32 percent of
the businessmen who did not emphasize the values of money or
status.

The importance of values on change of choice can be highlighted by comparing teachers who chose "people-oriented" values *plus* businessmen who selected "extrinsic-reward-oriented"
values with teachers and businessmen who failed to make the
choices characteristic of their groups (Table 48).

It may be observed that 57 percent of those agreeing with
the dominant value complex in their own groups remained in
their chosen occupations two years later compared with 27 percent of those who disagreed with the dominant value complex of
the occupational group. Since the combination of occupations
increases the size of our N's, the percentage differences here
are easily significant at the .01 level. In other words, occupational values do influence change of occupational choice,
but this influence is exercised in terms of the *norms* of the

group, *not in terms of specific values.*

Table 48
Dominant Value Complex among Teachers and Businessmen
and Change of Occupational Choice*

| People choosing teaching or business in 1950 who: | Teachers and Businessmen, 1950 | |
	Agreed with Dominant Value Complex, 1950	Disagreed with Dominant Value Complex, 1950
Remained in occupation, 1952	57%	27%
Changed occupation, 1952	43	73
N	(124)	(63)

* Percentage difference statistically significant at .01 level.

One of the most perplexing problems in the study of the occupational choice process is that of figuring out when a decision is actually a final decision. When has an ultimate crystallization taken place? If we are to improve our ability to predict whether or not a student making a certain choice will stick to it, we will have to give very careful consideration to the degree to which his values and his choice are in harmony or conflict.

Socio-economic ideology—It is not surprising that the literature on occupational choice has devoted little attention to the factor of socio-economic ideology. In many occupational areas, ideology is clearly irrelevant to the technical skills required for performance. However, while it may be that occupational activity for the engineer or the physicist does not differ materially in a capitalist or socialist society, the same cannot be said for the businessman. The style and ends of occupational action of the businessman depend entirely on the maintenance of capitalism, based on the principle of private investment for profit. Consequently, the businessman aspirant who, on the basis of certain group affiliations, holds a liberal socio-economic point of view is under cross-pressures. On the one hand, there are pressures rooted in the nature of the occupational activity pulling him in the conservative direction; on the other hand, he has adopted certain liberal convictions. Such a conflict must inevitably be reflected in some uncertainty of occupational choice.

For example, students were asked to agree or disagree with the following statement: "Democracy depends fundamentally on the existence of free business enterprise." Fifty-

three percent of those who agreed with the statement remained
faithful to their choice of business, while only 29 percent
of those who disagreed or were undecided failed to abandon
the field of business. Similar results were yielded when
students were presented with the following statement: "The
'welfare state' tends to destroy individual initiative."
Fifty percent of those who agreed with the statement were
businessman constants, compared with 28 percent of the disa-
agree-undecided group. Questions dealing with labor also
showed that the more liberal respondents were more likely to
shift away from the field of business. Confronted with the
statement, "The laws governing labor unions today are not
strict enough," 63 percent of those who agreed were unchang-
ing businessmen, compared with 35 percent of those who disagreed or were undecided. Finally, students were asked to a-
gree or disagree with the following statement: "Labor unions
in this country are doing a fine job." Fifty-five percent of
those who disagreed with the statement were constant businessmen, compared with 35 percent of those who disagreed or were
undecided. The number of respondents in each case is not
large, but the results are highly consistent.

It is possible to combine the answers to these four questions into a score of conservatism. Twenty-two people, or
26 percent of the businessmen, gave the conservative answer
to all four questions, while only one person, or 1.4 percent,
gave the liberal answer to all four questions. Thus it would
not be sound to speak of conservative and liberal businessmen, but rather to speak of more conservative and less conservative groups. When we compare those who gave consistently conservative answers with those who gave occasionally conservative answers, we can observe the impact of socio-economic ideology on change of occupational choice very clearly
(Table 49).

Table 49
Conservative Ideology and Change of Occupational Choice
among Businessmen*

People choosing business in 1950 who:	Conservative Ideology	
	Very Conservative	Not Very Conservative
Remained businessmen, 1952	73%	36%
Left business, 1952	27	64
N	(22)	(56)

* Percentage differences statistically significant at .01
level.

Businessmen who have a conservative ideology are significantly more likely to remain faithful to their occupational
choices over a two-year span than are those with more polit-
ically liberal convictions. Sixty-four percent of the latter, compared with 27 percent of the former, left the field
between the first and second interviews. Although ideology
may be irrelevant in many occupations, it is clearly an important factor in the decision to remain in the field of
business.

Commitment to Career

One set of factors fostering change of occupational
choice, we have seen, is any form of cross-pressures likely
to induce conflict in the individual. A qualitatively different set of factors producing change involves the degree
of *firmness* of the decision, or the intensity with which it
is held. Two factors influencing the firmness of a specific
occupational decision appear particularly important: (1) the
place of career in one's total value system, and (2) a certain personality orientation.

Major life satisfactions—"What three things or activities
in your life do you expect to give you the most satisfaction?"
This was the question asked of students in an effort to reveal
their basic value hierarchies. The alternatives presented
were: your career or occupation; family relationships; leisure-time recreational activities; religious beliefs or activities; participation as a citizen in the affairs of your community; participation in activities directed toward national
or international betterment. Respondents were instructed to
rank these alternatives in order of importance.

If a young person, looking into the future, expects to
obtain his major life satisfactions from his work, then it
is reasonable to describe him as "dedicated" to his career.
Are such people—the "career-dedicated" people—less likely
to change their occupational choices?

It is particularly appropriate to examine this question
among students selecting the field of medicine. The training
required for the study of medicine is so onerous, time-consuming, and costly that only a person firm and unwavering in his
occupational direction would be likely to resist the tempta-
tion to take an easier course.

Among the medical aspirants in 1950, twenty chose "career,"
27 chose "family," and five chose "others." Table 50 shows
that among those choosing "career," 80 percent still wanted to

be doctors two years later; among those choosing "family,"
however, only 33 percent still maintained their desires to be
doctors two years later—a difference of 47 percent.

Table 50
Main Source of Life Satisfaction
and Change in Choice of Medicine*

People choosing medicine in 1950 who:	Main Life Satisfaction	
	Career or Occupation	Family Relationships
Still chose medicine, 1952	80%	33%
Left medicine, 1952	20	67
N	(20)	(27)

* Percentage difference statistically significant at .01
level.

Those who left the profession, in addition, were even more
likely than those who remained to de-emphasize "career." For
example, of the 16 constants who in 1950 chose "career" as
their main life satisfaction, ten—or 63 percent—maintained
this choice in 1952; whereas of the four abandoners who chose
"career" in 1950, none maintained this choice in 1952. Similarly, of the nine constants who chose "family" in 1950, 56
percent had switched to "career" two years later; whereas,
among the 18 abandoners who chose "family" in 1950, only 22
percent had switched to "career."
Adherence to the field of medicine, therefore, appears to
be clearly related to the importance of career in one's total
life framework. Such dedication does not seem to be such an
influential factor in other occupational areas. It is likely
that students in college sooner or later recognize that the
study of medicine will be a difficult, time-consuming under-
taking. Those who tend to view their work simply as a way to
make a living in order to enjoy a satisfactory family life
would be more disposed to look for easier ways to fulfill
this aim. In other occupations, which involve less strain
and difficulty of training, the relative absence of dedication to career would be less likely to bring about change of
occupational choice.
Personality orientation—Those who have used the panel
method as an instrument of research have long sought to un-
cover some personality characteristic which might account for
some of the observed changes. Since personality was viewed
as a set of predispositions to behavior, there was specula-
tion as to whether certain people were predisposed to change

and others to remain constant *irrespective of the subject under investigation*. Obviously, it was recognized, all people
will vary in their degree of change, depending on what change
is under consideration. Yet it was felt that some people
were more "changeable" (the so-called "shifting personality")
and that this general predisposition accounted in part for
their shifts as panel members.

Whether we can discover the personality base for general
attitude change still remains an unsettled question. There
is one item of evidence in our study, however, which may suggest a direction which future research might pursue. The
concept behind this datum is a simple typological classifica-
tion. The first type of person is the one who tends to out-
line his life in broad strokes and to fit the details of day-
to-day life into that framework. He is the man who plans
carefully in advance and does not swerve from his established
path. For want of a better term, we might call this person a
"far-sighted" individual. The opposite type of person tends
to view matters in a day-to-day context and is discomfited by
thoughts of the long future. The extreme case would be the
"scatterbrain," the person who changes his mind from one mo-
ment to the next, who is like a leaf moving with every shifting breeze. In contrast to the first type, these people
might be characterized as the "myopics."

Our respondents were asked, "How important is it for you
to have your plans for the future clearly known to you in advance?" This question is phrased in general terms, covering
any life situation. It thus may serve as a crude index of
myopia and far-sightedness. Our thesis would be, of course,
that the far-sighted people, having made an occupational
choice, would be more likely to stick to it over a two-year
period than those who tended to adopt a shorter-range view.

Table 51 indicates that 71 percent of the teachers who
felt that knowing their plans in advance was not important
had changed their occupations during the two-year interval,
compared with 47 percent who considered it very important or
fairly important. Similarly, among the engineers who considered plans in advance unimportant, 29 percent had changed
their occupational decisions, compared with 17 percent of the
far-sighteds. Finally, 71 percent of the doctors who held
plans unimportant had changed their occupational choices,
compared with 40 percent of those who considered them important. The differences in the three occupations between the
myopics and far-sighteds are, respectively, 24 per cent, 12
percent, and 31 percent. It is important to note that the
question on "plans in advance" was phrased in the most general

terms; no special reference to the occupational area was im-
plied and the question was separated from the section dealing
with occupational information.

Table 51
Change in Occupational Choice by "Plans in Advance,"
among Teachers, Engineers, and Doctors*

Occupational Change	Importance of Plans in Advance	
	Very or Fairly Important	Not Very or Not at All Important
Teachers, 1950:		
Remained teachers, 1952	53%	29%
Changed occupation, 1952	47	71
N	(87)	(21)
Engineers, 1950:		
Remained engineers, 1952	83	71
Changed occupation, 1952	17	29
N	(125)	(58)
Doctors, 1950:		
Remained doctors, 1952	60	29
Changed occupation, 1952	40	71
N	(40)	(14)

* Percentage differences for combined occupations statistically significant at .01 level.

It would be both naive and pretentious to assume that we
could distinguish a complex personality constellation on the
basis of a single direct question, and no more respect should
be given this crude index than is due it. The results in
Table 51, however, certainly suggest the very interesting
possibility that the reason some people do not change their
occupational choices (or, by extension, their attitudes toward
many other things) may be their disposition to organize and
mark out their lives in long-range terms. Only future research can determine whether there is any basis in fact for
this challenging possibility.

Capacities and Decision Change

"We hold it as a basic fact that an individual, at least a
normal individual, cannot maintain an interest in an activity
or endeavor unless he is reasonably good at it." Thus do

Ginzberg and his associates[2] underscore the importance of
capacities in the selection and maintenance of an occupational choice.

But capacities are, by definition, always a guess, hidden
at present, only to be revealed in future abilities. No one
can know for certain how good a lawyer a student will make;
we can only make a more or less adequate guess of his future
behavior on the basis of our current knowledge of him.

Nevertheless, the broad principle of the importance of
capacities set forth by Ginzberg can hardly be questioned.
This is particularly true in the field of medicine. Medical
schools judge a college student's capacity to perform satisfactorily as a medical student largely on the basis of his
grades. Since this is common knowledge among students, we
would expect academic performance to serve as an important
self-filtering mechanism. However strong his original desire, a medical aspirant with an undistinguished academic
record must face the possibility of changing his occupational
choice. Of course, even academic performance could serve as
a measure of dedication, in the sense that those people who
really wanted to become doctors would work harder to obtain
better grades. However, such motivation is not sufficient in
itself. In our study we find that of the 26 medical aspirants who in 1950 had low grades (cumulative averages under 80
are considered low grades; averages over 80 are considered
high grades), only 27 percent still planned to be doctors two
years later; but, of the 28 aspirants who had high grades,
fully 75 percent still planned to become doctors, a difference of 48 percent (Table 52). Attaining and maintaining a
high academic average is not a sufficient condition for ad-
hering to one's choice of the field of medicine (there are
those with consistently good grades who nevertheless drop
out) but it generally appears to be a necessary condition.

Table 52
Cumulative Average and Change of Choice
of Medical Profession*

People choosing medicine in 1950 who:	Cumulative Average in 1950	
	Over 80	Under 80
Still chose medicine, 1952	75%	27%
Left medicine, 1952	25	73
N	(28)	(26)

* Percentage differences statistically significant at .01
level.

Persistence and Change of Social Pressures

The dominant mode of analysis traditionally employed in
survey research has involved the examination of the static
relationships among variables at a specified point of time.
Such a static relationship, however, is like a snapshot tak-
en with a still camera whose complete meaning becomes clearer when it is seen as part of a series in a motion picture.
This is particularly true in the study of occupational
choice. If we interpret some static relationship as the result of some system of pressures which has operated in the
past, then, if no other change has occurred, these pressures
would be expected to continue to operate in the future.
This would mean that, for the same group of people, a relationship obtaining at one point in time should have increased at a later point in time. We might label such a
phenomenon "the pattern of persistent pressures."
For example, our data reveal the obvious fact that people
from smaller communities are more likely than others to
select farming as an occupation. There are, however, those
from larger communities who wish to be farmers, and there
are, of course, many from small towns who do not make this
occupational choice. Nevertheless, we would expect the relationship between rural-urban residence and choice of farming to increase in the course of time. The person from the
larger community would have less contact with farmers and
would tend to receive less encouragement to enter this
field; relatively speaking, the opposite would be true of
those in small communities. Hence, we would expect that the
type of social milieu which operated to produce the original
relationship would continue to operate in the same direction
during the two-year period between interviews. The data are
shown in Table 53.

Table 53
Size of Home Community and Selection of Farming
as an Occupation, in 1950 and 1952

Occupa- tional Choice 1952	Size of Home Community								
	Under 2500			2500-200,000			Over 200,000		
	Occupational Choice, 1950								
	Farm	Other	Total	Farm	Other	Total	Farm	Other	Total
Farming	12	8	(20)	15	10	(25)	3	1	(4)
Other	6	96	(102)	21	513	(534)	12	242	(254)
Total	(18)	(104)	(122)	(36)	(523)	(559)	(15)	(243)	(258)

As we would expect, size of home community bears a clear-cut relationship to selection of farming as an occupation. In 1950, 15 percent of those from towns of under 2500 made this choice, compared with six percent of those from medium-sized communities, and six percent of those from cities of over 200,000. By 1952, this relationship had increased. Now 16 percent of the first group, four percent of the second group, and two percent of the last group, chose farming.

This progressively marked relationship between size of home community and occupational choice was attributable to two developments: (1) People from smaller towns who selected farming originally were more likely to maintain this choice than those from larger communities; (2) People from smaller towns who did not choose farming were more likely to switch to this field than were those from larger communities. For example, it may be observed that of the 18 small-town people choosing farming in 1950, 12—or 67 percent—maintained this choice in 1952; of the 36 people from medium-sized cities, 15—or 42 percent—did not change; and of the 15 large-city people choosing farming, only three—or 20 percent—failed to abandon this field. In other words, people from communities making this choice most frequently also maintained this choice most consistently.

Similarly, we find that eight percent of the people from small towns who had not chosen farming in 1950 made this choice two years later, compared with only two percent of those from medium-sized communities, and virtually none from large cities.

These data indicate that the original relationship is part of a continuing process which operates in a circular manner to strengthen this relationship. The small towner probably has had a good deal of contact with farmers and with others who deal with farmers; he is likely to have developed an interest and involvement in the problems of farming and to have considered it as an occupational alternative. His social milieu, of which the size of his home community is but an index, doubtlessly operates to channel and stimulate his interest in this occupation rather than in others. On the other hand, the urbanite who, let us say, has decided that he no longer wants to be an engineer is not stimulated by his social environment to consider farming as an alternative; few of his friends and relatives are involved in farming and the way of life associated with the occupation is likely to be considered strange and difficult. Thus, size of home community actually stands for a certain set of social pressures revolving about typical *interactions with others*. These pressures reinforce

the small towner's initial decision to enter farming and
cause the urbanite's decision to waver; in addition, farming
is presented as a prominent alternative to the small towner
who has changed his occupational choice, but not to the
person from the large community. In other words, the static
end result is the product of a dynamic interplay between the
individual and the environing social structure.

A similar pattern appears when we consider the changes in
occupational choices of men and women. Once again we will
start with an obvious static relationship—that men are con-
spicuously more likely to choose business as an occupation
than women. An examination of Table 54 reveals that this
relationship, which was strong in 1950, is still stronger in
1952.

Table 54
Expectation of Entering "Business" among Men and Women,
1950 and 1952

Expect to Enter, 1952	Expect to Enter, 1950					
	Men			Women		
	Business	Other	Total	Business	Other	Total
Business	17	61	(78)	-	4	(4)
Other	41	565	(606)	10	246	(256)
Total	(58)	(626)	(684)	(10)	(250)	(260)

In 1950, eight percent of the men, but four percent of
the women, expected to enter the field of business, a ratio
of 2:1; by 1952, the proportion of men expecting to enter
this field had increased to 11 percent; the proportion of
women had decreased to two percent, a ratio of 5.5:1.

The increase in this relationship is the product of a twofold process. Of the 58 men who planned to enter business
in 1950, 17—or 29 percent—still had this expectation in
1952. But of the 10 women who expected to enter this field
in 1950, everyone had changed her mind by 1952.[3] The role
pressures which had allowed so few women to choose business
in the first place evidently continued to operate on the
deviant women who chose business and eventually pushed even
more of them out of the field.

Similarly, only four women (two percent) who had not
planned to enter business in 1950 now made this choice in
1952, in contrast to 61 men (nine percent) who made this
switch. These data point to the likelihood that there is an
on-going social process calculated to filter men and women
into separate occupations.

Part of the socialization process of every society involves teaching children the pattern of role behavior appropriate to their sex statuses; among many other areas of action, this differential role behavior applies to the occupational area. For example, a boy's parents may encourage him
to enter the field of business but will not persuade his sisters to do so; the boy may be encouraged to follow in his
father's footsteps but not in his mother's; and so on. In
other words, the simple statement of a relationship between
sex status and occupational choice implies an extremely complex process of socialization and social role identification
whose multiple elements are only beginning to be identified.

The point is that people in a particular culture will
vary in their learning of the role and in their willingness
to play it. But the teaching of the social role goes on, and
sanctions in the form of ridicule and ostracism are employed
to press the deviant into role conformity. Thus the movement into occupations appropriate to one's sex status is not
a fact established once and for all but is part of a continuing process operating to produce a polarization in the choices
of certain occupations in the course of time.

The principle of persistent pressures would suggest that
if the factors which produced a relationship between two variables continued to operate to increase this relationship
over a period of time, then this relationship might eventually become perfect. The reason why it virtually never does
can be seen in the foregoing tables. In the first place,
there are countertendencies in operation[4] — women who do not
choose business on the first wave but do make this choice on
the second; men who choose business the first time but abandon
this choice two years later; and men who never seriously consider entering business either time. The panel method enables
us to single out these people in order to analyze the operation of such countertendencies.

There is no assurance, of course, that the relationship
between two variables will always increase; it will often, in
fact, decrease. Such a finding would then direct our attention to two questions: (1) Are there any reasons why the
pressures which originally produced the relationship should
now cease to operate? (2) Are there any new pressures, persistent in themselves, which exercise influence toward the
reduction of the relationship? For example, if we were to
find that the tendency for men and women to select different
occupations was decreasing, we might investigate whether students in college were being increasingly exposed to the doctrine of sexual equality and decreasingly exposed to the idea

of role differentiation. In this case, we might expect the relationship to be reduced through time, but, because of countertendencies, not to be entirely eliminated.

Finally, the relationship between two variables may be maintained at a stable level through time, but with a good deal of internal balancing within the system;[5] or there may be cyclical variations which suggest that once a relationship between two variables becomes too strong or too weak, new forces come into operation to restore it to its initial balance; and so on. Such speculations, of course, go far beyond our data, which consist of only two waves. They are presented only for the purpose of pointing out the idea that a relationship noted at a particular point in time is the result of a movement which is on the upgrade or downgrade or is on an even keel. If we wish to predict future behavior, of course, the meaning of a static relationship must often be viewed within such a time context.

CHAPTER VIII

THE ENDS AND MEANS OF OCCUPATIONAL ACTION

It has been said that if there is anything distinctively characteristic of the American value system, it is the emphasis placed upon success.[1] In a society stressing achievement rather than ascription, a man's[2] status and self-esteem are assumed to hinge to an important extent on his ability to get ahead in his field.

To know that an individual desires the goal of success, however, tells us nothing about the *means*—fair or foul—that he is willing to use to attain it. The problem of the cultural emphasis on monetary success and the institutionalized evasion of legitimate means for achieving it was raised some years ago by Robert K. Merton in his article "Social Structure and Anomie."[3] Merton pointed out that if the value of monetary success were very powerful but the legitimate means of achieving it severely restricted, then people might turn to normatively illegitimate means of attaining this goal. Those people who utilized dubious means for achieving success were characterized as "innovators." The belief that pressures actually did operate to promote this innovative pattern was expressed in Merton's statement that "contemporary American culture appears to approximate the polar type in which great emphasis upon certain success-goals occur, without equivalent emphasis upon institutional means."[4]

Similarly, Williams had indicated that people with strong drives for success (in the sense of money accumulation) may tend to violate the normatively sanctioned means for attaining it.

An overwhelming stress upon profit-making in organized economic enterprise quite obviously would tend toward an impatience with individual scruples, needs, and peculiarities and toward a calculating, impersonal use of others solely as a means toward the dominant end (of monetary acquisition).[5]

Thus, men are encouraged to strive for success, which according to these theorists means earning a good deal of money; however, the *legitimate* means for achieving this goal are not always the most *effective* means. For example, hard work, thrift, and initiative are viewed with approval within American society. It may not be *these* traits, however, but sharp dealing, manipulation, and unscrupulousness which enable a man bent on the goal of success actually to achieve it. Thus, the individual may confront this conflict: should he abandon the socially approved *goal* of success and engage in socially approved occupational behavior (*means*), or should he hold to the goal of success and accept the fact that he may have to use socially disapproved means for achieving it? Either alternative exposes him to the inevitable necessity of violating important social values.

This line of thought leads us to a number of interesting questions concerning the relationship between occupational ends and means. First of all, what is meant by success—is it exclusively a matter of earning money, or may one want success without valuing money highly? Does the desire for monetary success influence one's willingness to accept the use of dubious means in occupational practice? If a person who is very anxious to achieve monetary success tends to accept illegitimate means, does this necessarily indicate that he will *reject* legitimate ones, or is he, rather, willing to use *all* means—good, bad, or indifferent—to achieve his ends? These are the points to which we will direct our attention in the present chapter.

The Goal of Monetary Success

Most analysts of American values tend to assume that the desire for success is chiefly expressed in the desire to acquire a great deal of money. It is obvious, however, that the desire to get ahead and the desire to earn a good deal of money are not necessarily identical. A man may wish to achieve prominence by making important academic contributions, but he will scarcely cherish the illusion that he will ever make a great deal of money as a consequence. A young artist or poet may hope to achieve distinction in the realm of aesthetics, but will hardly expect such achievement to bring him actual wealth. In other words, people may wish to get ahead because of the prestige elements involved, because of the opportunities for self-fulfillment which the position affords, etc., without being motivated by the desire for wealth.

In the light of these considerations, it is interesting
to observe how close the relationship between the desire for
success and the desire for money turns out to be. As shown
in Table 55, 16 percent of those who were very anxious to
get ahead chose money as their prime occupational value, compared with one percent of those not anxious for success; and
50 percent of the former rated money highly important, compared with 10 percent of the latter.

Table 55
Desire to Get Ahead and Money as Occupational Value

| Money as Occupational Value | Important to Get Ahead in Life | | |
	Very Important	Fairly Important	Not Important
First choice	16%	6%	1%
High choice	34	21	9
Medium choice	43	61	51
Low choice	7	12	38
N	(584)	(445)	(106)

While the success-oriented person is more likely than others to value money, there are, in absolute terms, many persons
who desire success who do not stress money. But, it turns
out, there are *not* many money-oriented people who do not value
success. This can be shown by transposing the two variables
in Table 55; the results appear in Table 56. In other words,
the man who wants success does not always want money, but the
man who wants money always values success.

Table 56
Money as Occupational Value and Desire to Get Ahead

| "Important to get ahead" | Money as Value | | | |
	First Choice	High Choice	Medium Choice	Low Choice
Very important	77%	65%	44%	29%
Fairly important	23	31	47	40
Not very important or very unimportant	1	3	10	30
N	(115)	(299)	(564)	(134)

Further evidence that the strong desire for money is associated with a desire for success is afforded in response to the
question: "If you had your choice, which of the following
would you *most* like to be? (Check only one.)" The alternatives were: independent; successful; well liked. It will be

noted that as the importance of money as an occupational
value decreases, the proportion checking "successful" decreases markedly. At the poles, 65 percent of those selecting money as their first choice most wanted to be "successful," compared with only 18 percent of those who ranked money
as a low choice. The fact that less than one-fifth of those
who disdained money chose the "successful" alternative appears particularly significant. Monetary success appears to
be interpreted as the most common and important type of success, although it is not the only one.

Table 57
Money as Occupational Value and Desire to be "Successful"

"Which would you most like to be?"	Money as Value			
	First Choice	High Choice	Medium Choice	Low Choice
Successful	65%	51%	37%	18%
Independent or well-liked	35	49	63	82
N	(115)	(292)	(564)	(134)

The Goal of Monetary Success and the Means of Achieving It

Assuming that an individual is strongly imbued with the
desire for monetary success, what questionable means might he
adopt to achieve it? The range of improper ways of getting
ahead is, naturally, very wide. It will tend to vary, for
example, with the class background of the individual. Among
the working groups, it has been noted, more grossly illegal
means may be adopted—racketeering, other forms of criminal-
ity, prostitution, etc. However, "on the top economic levels, the pressure toward innovation not infrequently erases
the distinction between businesslike strivings this side of
the mores and sharp practices beyond the mores. As Veblen
observed, 'It is not easy in any given case—indeed it is at
times impossible until the courts have spoken—to say whether
it is an instance of praiseworthy salesmanship or a peniten-
tiary offense.'"[6]
Cornell students were asked to agree or disagree with the
following statement: "In order to get ahead these days...you
can't afford to be squeamish about the means you use." This
is a blunt statement regarding the relationship between success and the necessity for using institutionally dubious
means to achieve the desired end.

The first fact to be noted in Table 58 is that 70 percent
of the sample disagreed with this statement. This fact would
suggest that the idea expressed in it is *socially disapproved.*
The second, and more important, fact to observe is that those
who value money highly are distinctly more likely to agree
with the statement or to be undecided than are those who de-
emphasize money as an occupational value.[7] Fifty-five percent

Table 58
Money as Occupational Value and "Squeamish about Means"

| "Can't afford to be squeamish about means" | Money as Value | | | | |
	First Choice	High Choice	Medium Choice	Low Choice	Total Percent
Agree and undecided	55%	34%	25%	24%	30%
Disagree	45	66	75	76	70
N	(115)	(297)	(570)	(135)	(1,117)

of those who consider "the chance to earn a good deal of
money" their major occupational value fail to disagree with
the statement that "you can't afford to be squeamish about
the means you use," compared with 24 percent of those who
consider money as having little or no importance as an occupational value. Conversely, 45 percent of the former, compared with 76 percent of the latter, disagreed with the statement. This does not mean that all people desiring money as
an occupational value will necessarily sanction the use of
illegitimate means, but rather that they are more likely to
do so than are those who de-emphasize this value.

But the question may be raised: do they accept unscrupulous means because they want to make money or because they
want to get ahead in the world, irrespective of money? One
might imagine, for example, the case of a scientist improper-
ly appropriating another man's ideas, not for the purpose of
making money but with the aim of enhancing his own reputa-
tion; and cases of "playing politics" in governmental, business, and educational hierarchies are common knowledge. In
Table 59, however, it is shown that a strong desire for success does not necessarily lead to the acceptance of unscrupulous means; the person who does not value money tends to reject these means, irrespective of his desire to be successful. The key factor is the desire for money as such; irrespective of the desire to get ahead, the money-oriented man
tends to be more unscrupulous than the person unconcerned
with money.[8]

Table 59

Money as Occupational Value and "Squeamish about Means,"
among Those with Equal Desire to Get Ahead

	Important to Get Ahead											
	Money as Occupational Value											
	Very Important				Fairly Important				Not Important			
"Can't afford to be squeamish about means"	H 1*	H	M	L	H 1	H	M	L	H 1	H	M	L
Agree and undecided	56	36	27	22	50	27	24	22	-	(40)	22	22
Disagree	44	64	73	78	50	73	76	78	-	(60)	78	78
N	(88)	(195)	(247)	(53)	(26)	(94)	(263)	(60)	(1)	(10)	(53)	(42)

* H 1 refers to first choice, H to high (but not first) choice, M to medium choice, and L to low choice.

The approach we have adopted in this discussion has been
to question respondents about their attitudes directly. A
somewhat different method, designed to tap the situational
element, has also been employed. Specifically, we asked our
respondents how they would behave in a certain hypothetical
situation. This approach is illustrated by the following
rather lengthy story which appeared in our questionnaire:

HERE IS AN IMAGINARY
SITUATION. . . . . Mr. Winthrop is an old family
friend whom you know and like.
Business has been pretty bad for
some time now, and he is worried.

He manufactures a plastic gadget which could easily
compete with a rival steel product, except for one
thing:

A federal tax on Mr. Winthrop's product raises its
final price, so that it sells for almost the same
amount as the steel product.

Just last week, Mr. Winthrop learned that his steel
product competitors, in an effort to make sure that
this tax is retained, had hired a Washington lobbyist, notorious for shady tactics in persuading,
bribing, and even blackmailing congressmen to get
them to support his bills.

At a meeting of the Board of Directors of his
plant, Mr. Winthrop is offered the following solutions: Which single one would you counsel him to
follow? (Check one below)

Check one

_____ Go along as they have been.

_____ Start a high-powered publicity campaign to
secure public support against the tax.

_____ Hire a lobbyist, but be sure he is reputable.

_____ Hire a lobbyist, but let him use the same tactics as the steel lobbyist.

The third alternative presented, namely, the hiring of
the "reputable lobbyist," is difficult to classify either as
a socially approved or socially disapproved means. However,
it is possible to classify people who checked this alternative in terms of their responses to a related question:

In your opinion, is lobbying legal or illegal?
Check one: _____ Legal
_____ Illegal
_____ I don't know

We may assume that those people who advocate the use of a
"reputable lobbyist," but who feel that lobbying is illegal,
are actually sanctioning the use of socially disapproved
means, whereas those who consider lobbying legal probably do
not consider this means institutionally improper.

Thus, we will classify the following people as the group
sanctioning the use of illegitimate means to achieve monetary
success: those who advocate the use of a lobbyist who will
use the same methods as the steel lobbyist (persuading, bribing, or even blackmailing congressmen) plus those who recommend the use of a "reputable lobbyist," but consider lobbying
illegal or "don't know." All others will be classified as
those rejecting the use of disapproved means.

It will be noted in Table 60 that only a small proportion
of our sample (14 percent) advocated the use of those practices we have classified as socially disapproved. However,
among those selecting money as their first choice as an occupational value, 21 percent chose one of the disapproved practices, compared with seven percent of those who considered
this value irrelevant or even distasteful, a ratio of 3:1.
It seems plain that the money-oriented men have relatively
more unscrupulous attitudes than others.

Table 60
Money as Occupational Value and Advocacy of Use
of Socially Disapproved Business Practices

Would Counsel Winthrop to Use	Money as Value				
	First Choice	High Choice	Medium Choice	Low Choice	Total Percent
Practices that are:					
Approved (ethical)	79%	84%	86%	93%	86%
Disapproved (unethical)	21	16	14	7	14
N*	(74)	(216)	(376)	(100)	(766)

* Difference in N's due to the fact that this table is
based on 40 percent of the 1950 sample. Since no question on
desire for success appeared in the 1950 study, we cannot control here on this variable.

"Contacts" and inside influence as means of success—It is
often alleged that Americans feel that justice in the occupational realm consists in the matching of merit and reward.
The man at the top should be the one with the most intelli-

Table 61

Money as Occupational Value and Belief in Importance of Contacts, among Those with Equal Desire to Get Ahead

"Who you know… that counts"	Important to Get Ahead Money as Occupational Value											
	Very Important				Fairly Important				Not Important			
	H 1*	H	M	L	H 1	H	M	L	H 1	H	M	L
Agree and undecided	68	47	40	31	58	42	39	29	-	(50)	19	41
Disagree	32	53	60	69	42	58	61	71	-	(50)	81	59
N	(88)	(195)	(247)	(53)	(26)	(94)	(263)	(60)	(1)	(10)	(53)	(42)

* H 1 refers to first choice, H to high (but not first) choice, M to medium choice, and L to low choice.

gence or initiative or assiduity, not the one who has gotten
where he is by knowing the right people. If it is true, however, that an overwhelming stress on monetary success leads
to a relative indifference to the moral propriety of the
means to attain it, then we might expect the money-oriented
man to be relatively likely to sanction the use of "contacts"
and inside influence as a means for achieving success.

Those who value money highly, as Table 61 indicates, are
more likely to believe that "it's who you know more than what
you know that counts these days." Sixty-six percent of the
most strongly money-oriented men either agreed with or were
undecided regarding this statement, compared with 46 percent
who ranked money high, 38 percent who ranked it medium, and
32 percent who ranked it low.[9] Nor is this result due to the
money-oriented man's desire for success, for when we control
on the latter factor the relationship is still strong.[10]

The greater tendency for money-oriented people to stress
the importance of "contacts" for success is also illustrated
in another context. In the 1950 study, students were asked:
"What two qualities on this list do you think really get a
young person ahead fastest today? (Check two)" The alternatives were: hard work; having a pleasant personality;
brains; knowing the right people; good luck; being a good
politician.

Table 62 reveals that those people who value money highly
are more likely to emphasize the importance of "contacts"
than those who do not. Fifty-three percent of the former,
compared with 26 percent of the latter, insist that "knowing
the right people" is one of two qualities necessary for success. The alternative "being a good politician" is phrased
in such frankly cynical terms that very few people checked
it; nevertheless, more of the strongly money-oriented people
checked this response.

Table 62
Money as Occupational Value and Importance of "Contacts"
as Means of Success

| | | Money as Value | | |
Qualities that Get a Young Person Ahead	First Choice	High Choice	Medium Choice	Low Choice
Knowing the right people	53%	41%	36%	26%
Being a good politician	9	6	6	5
N*	(173)	(547)	(972)	(272)

* Based on total 1950 sample; since no question on desire
for success appeared in the 1950 study, we cannot control in
this table on this variable.

These data thus tend to point toward the following conclusion: people concerned with monetary success are more likely
than others to feel that institutionally dubious means are
necessary to get ahead. Relatively speaking, they feel that
moral scrupulousness is a deterrent to success and that contacts and inside dealings are more important than ability.
This finding is very clearly in accord with the analyses of
monetary success presented by Merton and Williams. However,
it is possible to view these data not simply as corroboration
of the theses presented by the above authors but also in
terms of certain other theoretical implications. In various
ways, direct and indirect, Merton and Williams imply that it
is the *structural imperatives* involved in the process of monetary acquisition which leads to the utilization of socially
illegitimate means. Williams states that the strong desire
for profit "tends obviously" to the use of these means;
Merton indicates that lack of capital or education makes monetary acquisition, using legitimate means, difficult. The
argument, then, would be that people know what the legitimate
means are, but that in the course of their work they find
that these means are ineffective for achieving the goal of
monetary success.

The point is, however, that we are dealing with students,
not mature adults; these are aspirants, not incumbents. They
can have had practically no personal experience with those
structural imperatives which presumably account for the relative acceptance of institutionally illegitimate means among
occupational practitioners. Why, then, do they behave as if
long experience had conditioned them to the idea that moral
virtue goes unrewarded in the world of work? Part of the answer probably lies in a factor we have already discussed,
namely, the process of anticipatory socialization. The
money-oriented student tends to internalize the behavioral
and attitudinal norms of the occupation prior to incumbency.
The cynical attitude toward success-means which the money-
oriented student brings to his work is less a question of
concrete occupational experience than it is a matter of prior
social learning, of prior internalization of socially re-
jected behavior patterns.

These results could not necessarily have been assumed
without reference to the empirical data. We might very well
have expected that young men preparing to travel the road to
monetary success would have expressed high-minded notions
about achieving success through hard work, perseverance,
initiative, and ingenuity. Only later, faced with the inexorable realities of occupational pressures, would they reluc-

tantly realize the necessity for also utilizing "contacts"
and skirting the fringes of legitimacy. Such does not turn
out to be the case. These people seem to be "socialized" before they enter their fields. They recognize and acknowledge
that the goal of monetary acquisition exerts pressure toward
the use of means which are *not* applauded by most people in
the culture *before they ever enter the field.* One of the
psychological functions of anticipatory socialization, incidentally, would be to limit the degree of internal conflict
which might otherwise be expected when an idealistic young
man faced the real pressures of occupational life.

Power as a Means of Achieving Monetary Success

Our focus thus far has been on the institutionalized evasion of social norms, stemming from the subordination of
means to ends. It is important to recognize, however, that
if a person is willing to utilize illegitimate means to
achieve success, this does not necessarily require him to
abandon approved means. He might be willing to use *all* means—
good, bad, and indifferent—to achieve his goals.

What are these approved means? There is often a tendency
to assume that any means which are not specifically disapproved are therefore socially satisfactory. This is true,
but it tends to overlook the important distinction between
those means which are "socially advocated" and those which
are "socially tolerated." Among the socially advocated means,
we would probably find such devices as hard work, thrift,
initiative, and ability. But there are other means which may
result in monetary acquisition, but which are neither illegitimate nor advocated. For example, a man may inherit a fortune;
this method of acquiring money is not disapproved, but it is
not thought to testify to his merit as much as if he gained
the money through hard work, sacrifice, and imaginative vision.[11] "Luck" would be a general example of a socially tolerated means—a man buys some property which turns out to have
oil on it. There is a range of means for achieving monetary
success which, although not illegitimate, nevertheless does
not fall within the framework of the traditionally virtuous
means. This, then, is our first question: What socially tolerated means are accepted by people bent on the goal of monetary success?

Our data indicate that the exercise of *power* is considered
an important means of attaining monetary success. Power is
one of the most fundamental forms of social interaction. In

the terms of Goldhamer and Shils, "A person may be said to
have power to the extent that he influences the behavior of
others in accordance with his own intentions."[12]   A very
clear expression of the belief that success depends upon the
exercise of power is contained in the following statement:
"In order to get ahead these days...you have to be able to
make people do what you want." Students were invited to
agree or disagree with this viewpoint.

Whether making people "do what you want" is to be accomplished through coercion, authority, or manipulation cannot
be determined; but the statement is explicit in indicating
that success depends upon influencing others in accord with
one's own intentions. Seventy-one percent of the money-
oriented students insisted that power was essential for success, compared with 46 percent of the non-money-oriented
people.[13] It would appear that there is a certain aggressive
interpersonal component involved in striving after money.

The reader may question our decision to classify power—
making people do what you want—as a *tolerated* means of success rather than as a *socially illegitimate* means. There are
both theoretical and empirical reasons for making this judg-
ment.

Table 63
Money as Occupational Value and Control of Others as Means

"Make people do what you want"	Money as Value				
	First Choice	High Choice	Medium Choice	Low Choice	Total Percent
Agree	71%	62%	47%	46%	54%
Undecided	7	12	17	14	15
Disagree	22	26	35	40	32
N	(115)	(300)	(570)	(134)	(1,119)

In the first place, it is obvious that in any large-scale
economic structure, power is inherent in the system of social
relationships. Every factory owner, every plant manager, every owner of a large commercial establishment, knows that he
must tell people what to do and must get them to do it if his
enterprise is to be successful. In addition, producers and
retailers must somehow induce consumers to purchase their
products. Power is thus a normal aspect of social interaction in the world of work.

On a more empirical level, we find that there is very
little relationship between the belief that the institutionally dubious means are essential for success and that power

is essential for success. For example, although we find a
high relationship between the belief that "in order to get
ahead these days...you can't afford to be squeamish about the
means you use" and "it's who you know more than what you know
that counts these days," we find only a small relationship
between either of these statements and the belief that "you
have to be able to make people do what you want."[14] The
weight of evidence would thus lean toward the conclusion that
power tends to be viewed as a tolerated, rather than a morally reprehensible, means of monetary success. Further evidence, however, would be required to establish this point
conclusively.

The tendency of the money-oriented man to view the exercise of power as one of the objective imperatives of success
is illustrated again if we focus on the non-authoritative aspect of power called manipulation—power through persuasion.
Our respondents were asked the following question: "When you
think of the qualities that will get a young person ahead in
the field you have chosen, which *two* of the following would
you say are most important?" The alternatives were: practical knowledge of theory and facts in your field; ability to
convince and persuade other people; lots of hard work and effort; organizing and administrative ability; personality;
high degree of intelligence or other special aptitude. The
notion of control and manipulation of others as essential
means of success is rather clearly expressed in the alternative "ability to convince and persuade other people."

Table 64
Money as Occupational Value and Belief that Success
Depends on "Ability to Convince and Persuade"

	Money as Value			
	First	High	Medium	Low
Qualities to Get Ahead	Choice	Choice	Choice	Choice
	(115)	(291)	(563)	(134)
"Ability to convince and persuade other people"	36%	26%	20%	19%

Those students primarily concerned with the occupational
value of money are almost twice as likely (36 percent to 19
percent) to claim that success in their fields depends on
their "ability to convince and persuade other people" as are
those who reject this value. This result, viewed in conjunc-
tion with the fact that the former are more likely to say
that success depends on the ability "to make people do what
you want," rather clearly suggests that those who value mone-

tary success feel that *an essential means for achieving it
is the control and manipulation of others for one's own ends.*

Thus far our emphasis has been on the means accepted as
essential for success by the money-oriented man. But what
about the individual who disdains money as an occupational
value? What means does he consider essential for success?
The answer seems to be that he believes satisfaction in the
work itself is a crucial factor. Seventy-six percent of
these people agreed (or were undecided) with the statement
that "in order to get ahead these days...you really have to
love your work," compared with 47 percent of those who placed
prime stress on monetary success. To those people who are
relatively unconcerned with money, work is probably both an
instrumental value and a goal value; the more anxious they
are to be successful, the more they insist that "to love your
work" is a prerequisite to success.

Socially Advocated Means of Occupational Success

We have seen that the money-oriented man tends to hold
distinctively different views regarding the illegitimate and
tolerated means essential for success. There is, in addition, another set of means which the society tends to define
as "good"; these are means which the individual *should* employ
in order to get ahead. If the money-oriented man is more
likely to accept dubious means of success, does this indicate
that he will necessarily reject advocated means?

While no definitive list of "socially advocated" means is
available, the exercise of the following characteristics appears to be generally applauded in the culture:

(1) Hard work   (2) Ability   (3) Initiative

When students were asked what two qualities would get a
young person ahead fastest in the fields they had chosen, the
money-oriented people appeared to differ very little from
others in their tendency to accept or reject socially advocated means of success (Table 65). As far as the traditional
virtue of "hard work" is concerned, the young man bent on
monetary success is no more (indeed slightly less) likely to
emphasize this characteristic as essential for success than
are other people. As far as "ability" is concerned, we might
consider this to be (1) practical knowledge of theory and
facts in your field; (2) organizing and administrative ability; or (3) high degree of intelligence or other special aptitude. None of these alternatives shows great and consistent differences.

There is no quality in the above list which clearly taps the element of "initiative." However, in a different section of the questionnaire, students were asked to agree or disagree with the statement: "In order to get ahead these days... you have to think of new ways of doing things." Agreement with this statement might represent an appraisal of the importance of initiative or imagination for success. Our results show virtually no differences in response to this question among people varying in their emphasis on the value of monetary success.

Table 65
Money as Occupational Value and Qualities
That Will Get Respondent Ahead in His Field

Qualities Which Get Person Ahead in Your Field	Money as Value			
	First Choice	High Choice	Medium Choice	Low Choice
Practical knowledge of theory and facts in your field	45%	55%	61%	51%
Lots of hard work and effort	34	30	40	40
Organizing and administrative ability	26	26	20	17
High degree of intelligence or other special aptitude	17	22	18	23
N	(115)	(291)	(563)	(134)

These very limited data, therefore, tend to suggest that people devoted to the value of monetary success are neither more nor less likely than others to embrace the traditional virtues of "hard work," "ability," and "initiative" as means of success. While these results may be partly an artifact of question wording or the list of alternatives presented, and should be viewed as highly tentative, the total effect is to suggest that the person who accepts institutionally dubious means does not necessarily reject legitimate ones.

It seems reasonable to conclude on the basis of these results that an important area for investigation in the sociology of occupations is the relationship between goal values and instrumental values. An increased specification of the range of disapproved, tolerated, and advocated means for achieving occupational ends would represent a most important step toward systematizing the knowledge in this area.[15]

CHAPTER IX

RELUCTANCE AND RESOLUTION

The Old Middle Class and the New

The economic history of the early days of the American republic revolves to a large extent about the activities of the old middle class. These were independent entrepreneurs—businessmen and farmers—whose economic fates hinged on the institution of private property. The life of the member of the old middle class was often difficult, but it also possessed certain attractions. It represented, first of all, *independence* from direct control by others, an advantage consonant with the emphasis on political freedom. It also fostered a maximal degree of ego-involvement in one's work. The property which the individual worked was his own. If it prospered, it was a tribute to his ability and assiduity. If it failed, the individual, rather than the system, was considered at fault. Finally, the possibilities for reward were virtually unlimited, and this reward was tangible and measurable and the source of multiple gratifications—money. The occupational model of the old middle class member thus came to be rooted in the American tradition as a type of cultural ideal.

The secular trend toward industrialization, economic concentration, and bureaucratization has brought about a decline in the old middle class and a tremendous upsurge in the group of propertyless white-collar workers called the new middle class.[1] These people have their talents, their training, and their personalities to put on the market, but they are not involved in investment for profit. At the higher levels, they are salaried professionals, managers, teachers, government workers, technicians, scientists—people selling their services to clients or to large bureaucratic organizations. These are the new middle class occupations which college students tend to enter.

In recent years the economic, political, and social lead-
ers of the society have tended to filter through the sieve
of the higher educational institutions, and increasingly
they have directed their educational efforts toward preparation for the occupations of the new middle class. To take
Cornell as an example, only one-fifth of the students realistically expected to enter one of the old middle class occupations—business, farming, or the free professions (Table
66). Many of these people were planning to become farmers
and were attending Cornell's large and well-known College of
Agriculture. About three-quarters of the students expected
to be salaried employees, selling nothing but their skills,
and a few expected to enter the family business.

Table 66
Kind of Firm or Outfit after Completion of Education

Kind of Firm or Outfit	Like Best to Work in	Realistic- ally Expect to Work in
Own business or own farm	29%	11%
Own professional office	17	8
Educational institution	11	13
Social agency	3	4
Other non-profit organization	2	2
Government bureau or agency	5	7
Family business or enterprise	3	6
Private firm, organization, or factory	25	44
Other	2	2
Probably will not work	2	3
N	(1066)	(1066)

If the contemporary student does not expect to enter private entrepreneurial occupations, however, this does not mean
that the old middle class ideal has completely faded from
the picture. When members of our Cornell sample were asked:
"If you could have your own choice in the matter, what kind
of FIRM or OUTFIT would you like best to work in after you
finish your schooling?" 29 percent said "own business or own
farm" and 17 percent "own professional office." But when
they were asked: "Now, aside from your own preference in the
matter, what kind of firm do you think you are realistically
most likely to end up working in?" only 11 percent said "own
business or own farm" and 8 percent "own professional office."
Thus, whereas nearly half of the students hold to the traditional cultural ideal of occupational independence, only a

fifth actually expect to achieve it. Contrariwise, 45 percent of the students actually *expected* to enter a "private
firm, organization, or factory" compared to only 25 percent
who *desired* it. The attractions of the old middle class occupations are still alluring, but the new generation makes a
resigned bow to reality.

Since the old middle class occupations basically involve
working for oneself in some enterprise, it has traditionally
been assumed that capital or credit was essential to the
young man entering the economic arena. Yet in view of the
students' expectations, it is not surprising to find that
only very rarely does the contemporary college student look
forward to scraping together some capital and going into
business for himself. Students were given a list of 16
characteristics which "will get a young person ahead in the
field you have chosen." It turns out that the quality of
"having capital or access to it" ranks next to the lowest on
this list; it is chosen by only 12 percent of the students,
compared, for example, with the 62 percent who checked "an
ability to get people to like you" and the 65 percent who
selected "understanding of other people." Thus, the old
middle class ideal of occupational independence—being one's
own boss, setting one's own pace, assuming responsibility—
still prevails strongly, but the occupational expectations
tend to accord more closely with the historical fact of the
growth of large-scale organizations designed to cope with
the economic and occupational tasks of the society.

But if there is a relatively widespread conflict between
aspirations and expectations as far as type of firm or outfit is concerned, this is much less true when we consider
the choice of specific occupations. Among the Cornell respondents, 76 percent wanted to enter the same occupations
they realistically expected to enter,[2] while the remaining
fourth did not expect their occupational desires to come
true. Students might wish to enter their own business, but
they expected to work for someone else. Future lawyers
might hope to enter their own law office, but many expected
to work for legal firms, businesses, or government agencies.

In which occupation was the conflict most acute? In order to clarify the basis of comparison, we have computed an
index of *anticipated frustration* by dividing the number entering each field *reluctantly* (*i. e.*, they would "most like"
to go into a different occupation) by the total number expecting to enter that field. The results are shown in Table
67.

It will be noted in Table 67 that the three occupations
with indices of anticipated frustration exceeding .40 fall

within the general field of business; namely, real estate-
finance, business (unspecified), and sales-promotion. In
other words, business appears to draw a considerably larger
proportion of reluctant recruits than other fields. The im-
pression one obtains is that people are more likely to view
business as a sorry second-best rather than an area of gold-
en opportunity. If there is anything "calling" the middle
class American youth, it is not the voice of business.

Table 67
Index of Anticipated Frustration among Occupations
(in Rank Order)

Occupation	Index Anticipated Frustration	Total Expecting to Enter Occupation
Real estate-finance	.53	(17)
Business, unspecified	.48	(115)
Sales-promotion	.40	(121)
Architecture	.31	(78)
Government work	.30	(53)
Teaching	.26	(377)
Personnel	.25	(80)
Journalism-drama	.25	(65)
Advertising-public relations	.24	(21)
Social work	.24	(46)
Natural science	.23	(129)
Law	.22	(88)
Social science	.19	(59)
Engineering	.15	(404)
Farming	.15	(240)
Hotel	.15	(156)
Art	.14	(29)
Medicine	.07	(158)
		(2,298)

At the other end of the list, the occupation drawing the
smallest number of reluctant recruits is medicine. In view
of the sacrifice in time and training that is required of
them, this expression of high motivation on the part of medical aspirants is undoubtedly highly functional. It is
plain that very few people entering the field of medicine
would prefer an alternative occupation.

The low index of frustration in the field of art is rather self-explanatory; very few people are "forced" or "press-
ured" into entering the world of art against their wills.

Indeed, the association of the values of creativity and self-expression with the field of art virtually demands, for productive work, that this occupation be chosen voluntarily and enthusiastically.

It would be a matter of interest to examine these various occupational groups in order to account for the differential degrees of anticipated frustration. For example, the reasons for the large proportions of reluctant teachers and government workers demand explanation. In this chapter, however, we intend to focus on one occupational group, the group with the highest index of occupational frustration; namely, the businessmen (those men choosing business [unspecified], real estate-finance, and sales-promotion). Our aim is to examine certain of the factors that are responsible for the gap between aspirations and expectations in the field of business.

A Framework for Deviant Case Analysis

Methodologically, the most convenient way of approaching this problem is through the use of a typology. Since we are dealing with two dimensions, namely, aspirations and expectations, it is possible to construct four types in terms of the agreement between these two dimensions. The first consists of those people who *desire* to enter the field of business and also *expect* to enter it; this group will be called the *willing businessmen*. The second consists of those who neither wish to enter one of the business fields nor expect to enter them; these are the *non-businessmen*. The other two types experience some conflict between their aspirations and expectations. One of these groups expects to go into the field of business but actually would prefer to enter some other occupation; we will refer to this group as the *reluctant businessmen*. The other deviant case consists of those people who would really like to enter one of the business fields but do not expect to do so; these are the *frustrated businessmen*. Since business is essentially a male field, we will focus our attention on the men in our sample. How are these four types distributed in the sample? (Table 68)

Our data indicate that 121, or 6.1 percent are willing businessmen; 91, or 4.6 percent are reluctant businessmen; 25, or 1.3 percent are frustrated businessmen; and 1759, or 88.0 percent are non-businessmen. It would have been interesting to learn why the frustrated businessmen failed to enter the occupational fields they desired. Unfortunately, the number of people falling into the category was very

small, and analysis of these people revealed that our data
were inadequate to account for their behavior. Hence, we
have omitted this group in our subsequent analysis and
focussed our attention on the reluctant businessmen.

Table 68
Aspirations and Expectations toward Business, among Males

| | | Field of Business | | |
		Desired	Not Desired	Total
Field of Business	Expected	121	91	212
	Not expected	25	1759	1784
	Total	146	1850	1996

In principle, an explanation of the plight of the reluctant businessmen would require answers to the following four
questions:

1. Why do they *not want* to enter the field of business?
2. Why do they *want* to enter other fields?
3. Why do they *not expect* to enter other fields?
4. Why do they *expect* to enter the field of business?

The usefulness of a model of this sort is not that it in-
sists that all these questions be answered separately, since
a reason for doing something may also be an adequate reason
for not doing its opposite, but that it provides a framework
for all possible explanations and indicates the groups to be
compared. As a matter of fact, our data are inadequate to
answer question 2. Hence, we will seek to provide partial
answers to the other three questions.

The Reluctant Businessman

Why is he reluctant (i. e., why does he not want to enter
the field of business)?—Our data indicate that one reason
the reluctant businessman is unhappy about going into business is that, relatively speaking, his socio-economic ideology tends to be at loggerheads with the principle of unrestricted private investment for profit. Two Guttman scales,
designed to reflect political liberalism and conservatism,
were set up: one was called the "big-business minded" scale,
and the other the "socialism-planning" scale.[3] How do the
Reluctants compare with the Willings on these scales?
    As Table 69 shows, 22 percent of the Reluctants rank high
on the scale of "business-orientation," compared with 45 percent of the Willings; conversely, at the low end of the scale

Table 69
*Attitude toward Business as an Occupation
and "Business Orientation"

| | Attitude toward Business | | |
"Business orientation"	Reluctant Businessmen	Willing Businessmen	Non-Businessmen
High pro-business	22%	45%	30%
Intermediate	21	17	23
Low pro-business	57	38	48
**N	(42)	(53)	(517)

* Percentage differences between Reluctants and Willings statistically significant at the .05 level.

** The reduction in size of N's is due to the fact that the "business orientation" score has been gang-punched on a random 40 percent of our total 1950 sample.

the ratio of Reluctants to Willings is 1.5:1. It should be noted that the Reluctants have an even stronger ideological opposition to big business than the mass of students who do not expect to enter business at all. The Willings have the strongest ideological commitment to the system of free enterprise and big business. Similarly, on a score dealing with favorableness toward government planning or receptivity to socialist measures, people who expected to enter various occupations responded in the following way:

Table 70
*Attitude toward Business as a Vocation
and Socialism-Planning Score

| | Attitude toward Business | | |
Socialism-planning score	Reluctant Businessmen	Willing Businessmen	Non-Businessmen
Anti-socialism-planning	57%	85%	63%
Pro-socialism-planning	43	15	37
**N	(42)	(53)	(517)

* Percentage difference between Reluctants and Willings statistically significant at the .01 level.

** Socialism-planning score gang-punched on random 40 percent of entire sample.

Eighty-five percent of the Willings manifest opposition to socialism-planning, as reflected in the score, compared with 57 percent of the Reluctants, a difference of 28 percent.

The agreement of these data with the results of the "business orientation" score leaves little doubt that ideological opposition to business is a factor conducive to reluctance to enter the field.

As far as the Reluctants are concerned, we may say that people who manifest moral horror at the rules of the game cannot be good players. It is analogous to a man who hates to inflict pain becoming a prize-fighter or a pacifist entering military service as a profession.

Why is he a businessman (*i. e.*, why does he actually expect to enter the field of business)?—The first reason that comes to mind is that family pressure or inducements have been operating to draw the Reluctant into business. We know from the work of Centers[4] and others that sons are more likely to enter their fathers' general occupational areas than any other single occupational area. Our expectation would be, therefore, that the youth whose father is in business has induced his son, through whatever form of persuasion, to go into business too. Since the Reluctants expect to enter business, whereas the non-businessmen do not, and since we are concerned with those factors contributing to expectations, the critical comparison must be between these two groups. What are their fathers' occupations?

It will be noted in Table 71 that 71 percent of the Reluctants, compared with 61 percent of the Willings and 38 percent of the non-businessmen, have fathers who are proprietors. Whether the parents exert pressure covertly or overtly, whether the influence is exercised by simply smoothing the occupational path of the young man, whether it is "simply assumed" that the young man will go into business with his father, the Reluctants are doubtlessly exposed to greater parental influence thrusting them toward business than are the non-businessmen.

Table 71
*Attitude toward Entering Business by Father's Occupation

Father's Occupation	Attitude toward Entering Business		
	Reluctant Businessmen	Willing Businessmen	Non-Businessmen
Professional	9	12	30
Farm owner	2	1	11
Proprietor	71	61	38
All other occupations	18	26	22
N	(65)	(82)	(380)

* Percentage differences of Reluctants whose fathers are proprietors and non-businessmen whose fathers are proprietors statistically significant at .01 level.

While it is reasonable to assume that fathers who are businessmen would be more likely than other people to influence
their sons to enter business, either by direct persuasion or
through indirect devices (such as familiarizing their sons
with the field), it is likely that they would do so only if
they themselves had been successful. If a man has had an unsuccessful career it would, in general, be rather unfatherly
to wish his son the same ill fate. In order for the hypothesis of family pressure to be maintained, therefore, it would
be necessary to show that the Reluctants' fathers are economically successful people.

Table 72
Attitude toward Business and Father's Income

"About how much was your father's income last year as far as you know...?"	Attitude toward Business		
	Reluctant Businessmen	Willing Businessmen	Non- Businessmen
Less than $3,000	4	6	7
$3,000-$5,000	11	10	19
$5,000-$7,500	14	13	17
$7,500-$10,000	15	11	12
$10,000-$20,000	16	23	15
$20,000-$30,000	8	8	5
Over $30,000	9	7	2
Don't know; no answer	22	23	23
N	(91)	(120)	(533)

Table 72 indicates that, compared with the other members of
the sample, the Reluctants' fathers are relatively well-to-do
people. Seventeen percent of them had earned over $20,000
during the previous year, compared with 15 percent of the
Willings' fathers, and only 7 percent of the non-businessmen's
fathers. Conversely, 29 percent of the Reluctants' fathers,
29 percent of the Willings' fathers, but 43 percent of the
non-businessmen's fathers earned under $7,500. It would thus
be understandable that the Reluctants' fathers, who are themselves relatively successful businessmen, would be particularly likely to draw their sons into the field of business.

These data, incidentally, demonstrate the unlikelihood that
lack of money has prevented many Reluctants from entering the
professions they desire. Indeed, we find that the Reluctants
come from families wealthier than those of the students who
expect to become doctors, and practically no field exceeds
medicine in costliness of training. It is therefore particularly unlikely that many Reluctants would be debarred from

other fields for lack of funds.

Why is he not a "non-businessman" (*i. e.,* why does he not expect to enter the field he desires)?—Although family pressure may operate to draw the Reluctant toward business, he still might not yield to that pressure if there were no factors keeping him out of the field he wanted to enter.

There are four occupations desired quite frequently by the reluctant businessman. These are: medicine, science, teaching, and journalism-drama. Success in training for the first three of these is thought by the students to be related to "brains"—though the more accurate formulation would be academic proficiency. How does the academic proficiency of the Reluctant compare with that of the person who actually expects to become a doctor, a scientist, or a teacher? (Table 73)

Table 73
*Reluctant Businessmen and Prospective Doctors,
Scientists, and Teachers by Cumulative Average

Cumulative Average	Reluctant Businessmen	Prospective Doctors	Prospective Scientists	Prospective Teachers
Under 80	67	33	40	52
Over 80	33	67	60	48
N	(91)	(117)	(88)	(111)

* Percentage differences between Reluctants and doctors statistically significant at .01 level; between Reluctants and scientists at .01 level; and between Reluctants and teachers at .05 level.

The results are clear-cut. The reluctant businessmen have, relatively speaking, a strikingly unsuccessful academic record. While only one-third of the Reluctants have cumulative averages over 80, two-thirds of the doctors, three-fifths of the scientists, and nearly one-half of the teachers hold these high grades. This result suggests rather strongly one major reason why the Reluctants desiring to enter other professions fail to do so. They have reason to feel that they do not have the academic ability for other more desirable careers.

Part of the reason for the Reluctant's poor grades is that he takes his school work less seriously and is relatively confused or uncertain regarding his academic interests. The Reluctant admits that he cuts classes more often than other students. For example, 47 percent of the Reluctants, compared

with 57 percent of the prospective scientists, 58 percent of
the prospective doctors, and 63 percent of the prospective
teachers, cut classes "less often than most students you
know." (Table 74)

Table 74
*Reluctant Businessmen and Prospective Doctors,
Scientists, and Teachers by Cutting Classes

"Do you think you cut classes more or less often than most students you know...?"	Reluctant Business- men	Pro- spective Doctors	Pro- spective Scientists	Pro- spective Teachers
More often	15%	8%	16%	4%
About as often	38	34	27	32
Less often	47	58	57	63
N	(92)	(118)	(89)	(117)

* Percentage difference between reluctant businessmen who
cut classes "less often" and other occupations combined is
statistically significant at the .05 level.

Similarly, the Reluctant is less likely than others (Table
75) to say that he is "very interested" in his major field of
study (only 30 percent of them check this alternative, compared with 56 percent of the non-businessmen, and is more
likely (Table 76) to have changed, or to be considering
changing, his major field of study (51 percent of the Reluctants compared with 29 percent of the non-businessmen); his
inferior academic performance is thus quite understandable.

Table 75
*Attitude toward Business
by Feelings about Major Field of Study

"How do you feel about your major...?"	Attitude toward Business		
	Reluctant	Willing	Non-
	B u s i n e s s m e n		
Don't know what it is like yet	8%	7%	6%
Haven't chosen one yet	7	4	4
Very interested in it	30	45	56
Fairly interested in it	41	33	28
Not interested in it	8	4	1
Not sure how I feel about it	7	8	5
N	(88)	(119)	(522)

* Percentage differences between Reluctants who are "very
interested" and non-businessmen statistically significant at
.01 level, and between Reluctants and Willings at .05 level.

Table 76
*Attitude toward Business
and Change of College Major (1952)

"Have you changed your major field of study..."	Attitude toward Business		
	Reluctant	Willing	Non-
	B u s i n e s s m e n		
No, and not considering changing	48%	63%	71%
No, but am considering changing	17	4	7
Yes, have changed my major	34	33	22
**N	(29)	(111)	(291)

* Percentage differences between Reluctants who are not considering changing and non-businessmen significant at .05 level; barely misses at .01 level.

** The smallness of the N's is due to the fact that this table is taken from the 1952 study, which consisted of a smaller sample than the 1950 study. Unfortunately, this question did not appear in the earlier study. The non-business group represents a random 30 percent selected for purposes of comparison.

These data suggest, then, that the Reluctant is relatively uncertain about, and uninterested in, his school work, particularly his major field of study; he cuts classes more often than others and ends up with lower grades. But high grades may be considered essential for the fields the Reluctant would like to enter, and he may thus have to relinquish his occupational desires.

It is also possible that his confusion and poor work in school is a *result* of the conflict about his occupational future. Uncertain about his career and dubious about the utility of his courses, he may feel it is futile to take school work seriously. In this case, a circular pattern may ultimately develop. A youth with average grades may feel that high grades are necessary for the field he desires; lacking such grades, he feels there is little point in studying, his grades decline further, and his chances of entering his desired field become increasingly remote. It is possible that this pattern may be operating among some of the Reluctant businessmen.

The Outcome of the Conflict

Two instances of a gap between occupational aspirations and expectations have been cited; one, that of people who hold old middle class values but expect to enter new middle class occupations; the second, that of students who would like to enter non-business fields but expect to go into business. Such a result points to a social problem of some seriousness. From the point of view of the individual, he faces the prospect of spending the most productive hours of his remaining life doing work he pro'-ably will not enjoy or, at least, about which he has seriou; reservations. From the viewpoint of the economic structure, the possibility exists that a substantial number of poorly motivated people may be inducted into the work force who may do their jobs perfunctorily and without inspiration. We would be led astray in our analysis of such problems, however, if we failed to take account of the tendency of the human mind, in the course of time, to devise ways of reducing inner conflict.

This can be demonstrated by examining the outcome of the Reluctant's conflict. Will he eventually go into business? In terms of his testimony, the answer by and large is that he will not. Of the panel members who were Reluctants in 1950 we find that, two years later, fully four-fifths of them had given up the idea of going into business; this is in striking contrast to two-fifths of the Willings who changed their occupational expectations (Table 77).

Table 77
*Attitude toward Business and Change of Occupational Choice

Change of Occupational Expectations	Attitude toward Business, 1950	
	Reluctant Businessmen	Willing Businessmen
Remained in business, 1952	20%	61%
Left business, 1952	80	39
**N	(46)	(44)

* Percentage differences statistically significant at .01 level.
** Small N's are due to the limited size of the panel.

Despite the fact that the Reluctants' fathers tended to be in business, and despite the family pressure that probably was applied in some fashion, the sense of "free choice" is so strong in the young American male that if he really does not want to go into business, he will change his occupational expectations in the course of time. The social and psychological dysfunctions stemming from the conflict between aspirations and expectations are, at least with regard to this occupational area, largely eliminated.

Now, let us return to the question of those who wished to
be independent entrepreneurs or professionals, but expected
that they would end up as salaried employees. Here the reality appears to be of a tougher and less malleable sort, for
the objective evidence probably becomes increasingly clear
that occupational independence is a rare phenomenon. What
happens under these circumstances is shown in Table 78.

Table 78
Desire and Expectation of Entering Own Business, Farm,
or Professional Office, 1950 and 1952

1952	1950				
	Desire; Expect	Desire; Not Expect	Not Desire; Expect	Not Desire; Not Expect	Total
Desire—Expect	80	31	4	21	(136)
Desire—Not Expect	34	85	7	77	(203)
Not Desire—Expect	2	4	-	6	(12)
Not Desire—Not Expect	37	134	9	413	(593)
Total	(153)	(254)	(20)	(517)	(944)

The first point to be noticed is that a decrease in conflict has occurred during the two-year span. In 1950, there
were 254 people who would have liked to be occupationally independent but did not expect to be, and 20 people who did not
desire their own outfits but did expect to enter them. By
1952, the number in the former group had decreased to 203,
and in the latter group to 12. In other words, 29 percent of
the students were in conflict in 1950, but two years later
this proportion had decreased to 23 percent.

How had this decrease in conflict come about? First of
all, the problem had been resolved by decreasing *both* the desire and expectation of entering one's own enterprise or
office and increasing both the desire and expectation of
working for someone else. In 1950, 407 students *desired* to
enter their own firms; in 1952, only 339. In 1950, 173 students *expected* to be occupationally independent; in 1952,
only 148. Another way of putting this is to note that in
1950, 517 students neither desired nor expected to be their
own bosses, whereas by 1952 this number had increased to 593.

These data also furnish another example of the observation
that under those conditions in which the reality is perceived
as "tough," the value system tends to adjust to it. This can
be seen by taking those people who were initially inconsistent

and observing the form their consistency assumed (Table 79).
In 138 cases, the values changed to accord with the expectations, whereas in 40 cases the expectations changed to agree
with the values. The bulk of the people were those who said
they no longer *desired* to enter one of the "old middle-class"
occupations.

Table 79
People Whose Desires and Expectations Were Inconsistent
in 1950 Who Became Consistent in 1952

	1952	
1950	Desired and Expected Own Business*	Did Not Desire and Did Not Expect Own Business
Desired own business; did not expect it	31	134
Expected own business; did not desire it	4	9

* Includes own business, own farm, or own professional office.

In the instances studied here, then, we find that, given a
cultural value which is faced by an inexorable economic reality, the individual moves toward the conclusion that the value
is not really important; ultimately he no longer "wants" that
which he does not expect to get. From the viewpoint of the
sociology of knowledge, these data demonstrate rather well
how "ideas" (in this case, values) change in the course of
time to accord with objective social conditions (although in
some cases, as has been noted, the perception of the objective situation may change to agree with the values). In
either case the tendency is toward the reduction of psychological tension which has been engendered by the conflict between social values and economic conditions.

It would be an error to assume, however, that the human
mind is infinitely flexible in avoiding culturally-induced
conflicts. Even after the two-year span, there still remained 23 percent of the students who would have desired to
be occupationally independent, but expected to be salaried
employees; many of them had, in fact, developed this desire
between 1950 and 1952. Whether these people ultimately resolve their conflicts, and whether, among those who do not
resolve them, there is a development of occupational malad-
justments, are questions which can only be answered by future
research.

CHAPTER X

CONCLUSION

Social Contribution and Individual Satisfaction

It is one thing to ask how the student makes up his mind about his career and quite another to ask how he will get along in his field once he starts working. In the absence of a longitudinal study following the student from his college days through his work career, we can only speculate on the possible implications of our data for the productiveness and satisfaction of the student's future work. Let us first look at the bright side of things—what positive signs are contained in our data which favor the student's chances of making a positive contribution to society in his work, finding his work a rewarding experience, and adjusting to it without excessive conflict?

The first fact to be noted is that, by and large, the student enters his occupation *willingly*. In our nationwide survey, as we noted in Chapter IX, 78 percent of the students desired to enter the occupations they actually expected to enter. This does not mean, of course, that these people have been blithely free of occupational conflict during the entire course of their college careers; rather, it indicates that, in the course of time, they come to "want" what they realistically expect to get. Not only are their occupational aspirations quite realistic at the outset (very few set their sights on becoming President of the United States, business tycoons, or immortal scientists), but they continue to modify them in accordance with the brittleness of reality. There may remain some longing backward glances at the old middle class occupations, but, as the student advances in college, he increasingly wants to enter the new middle class field that he realistically expects to go into (Chapter IX). Similarly, among those students whose occupational values and choices are in conflict, there is a tendency either to switch to an occupation in which they feel they can satisfy their values, or to select occupational values which they feel their chosen fields can satisfy (Chapter II). Such "malleability of wants" and "malleability of reality" have the effect of making them more contented, more satisfied, more willing to enter their fields. There are, of course, a goodly number of reluctant recruits, and their prospects for a good occupational adjustment are not bright. Our data suggest, however, that most of the students enter their fields with the best possible attitude for adjustment—the attitude that the fields they are going into are the ones they really desire to enter.

A second factor which may have positive consequences for the economic structure is the strong emphasis on "productive" values which the student tends to bring to his work. As we observed in Chapter II, most students want a job in which they can use their "special abilities or aptitudes" or in which they have an opportunity to be "creative and original." And as the data in Chapter VI indicated, the emphasis upon these values continues to increase during the course of their college careers, while the concern with the extrinsic rewards of work (e. g., security) tends to wane. In other words, there is a strong and increasing tendency for the college student to ask, "How can I expend my highest talents and abilities in my work?" rather than, "What will they give me for working?" Some people may devote their fullest, most productive talents to their work without requiring much in return, whereas others grudge every ounce of effort which is not directly compensated. Since every society has limited resources in comparison to people's potential needs, the "creative" approach to work is clearly advantageous to the economic system. There are possible disadvantages to this approach, too, as we will see in a later section. However, it seems reasonable to assume that the individual who gives his best talents to his work and shows relatively little concern with the rewards he receives is likely to adjust well to his job.

Thirdly, the ease of adjustment to one's occupational role is likely to be promoted by the process of anticipatory socialization. One potential problem involved in moving from the status of student to that of occupational incumbent is that there will be a certain amount of awkwardness and inefficiency in switching statuses. It might take some time for the individual to internalize the new status as an element of his self-picture and to learn the appropriate role behavior. Even as a student, however, the individual is learning to think of himself as a doctor or lawyer or teacher, and is rehearsing, either in his mind or overtly, the behavior appropriate to that status. The data in Chapter II suggested, for

example, that the student may change his current values to
accord with those which he believes will be appropriate for
his chosen occupation. If the individual correctly learns
the values, attitudes, and behavior appropriate for the occupational status he expects to occupy, and if he begins to internalize them, then he becomes "partly" a doctor or engineer
while still in college. The transition to the actual occupational status, then, can be accomplished relatively smoothly.

A fourth factor fostering occupational adjustment and satisfaction is related to the earnings expectations of college
students. Havemann and West,[1] in their study of college
graduates, showed that the graduates from wealthier families
tended to earn more than the poorer college people. This
finding corresponds, as we have seen in Chapter V, to the
contemporary student's earnings expectations. Not only do
earnings expectations of students increase with family
wealth but more of the wealthier students place high value on
the chance to earn a good deal of money. If there is no
change in economic conditions in the future, then, it is
likely that those who expect to earn a good deal of money
will actually do so and those who do not have this expectation will not. Such expectations seem likely to minimize
dissatisfaction with the monetary rewards these people will
eventually receive.

Finally, occupational adjustment may be fostered by the
wide range of occupational values and occupational choices
available to the student. Whatever the individual's particular hierarchy of values—whether he be chiefly concerned with
making money, or using his talents, or having good interpersonal relations, or having freedom or adventure—he believes
that he can satisfy it in some kind of work. *If* he is cor-
rect, this would mean that the occupational structure is
broad enough to satisfy the different, special, and unique
needs of a wide range of individuals. This hypothesis gains
strength from the fact that there are such a vast number of
occupations available, many of which vary a good deal in
their characteristics, and that the social norm of free
choice prevails. Unlike a caste society, in which the individual's occupation is marked out for him at birth, the
American occupational structure provides a good opportunity
for the individual to find that occupation which suits his
special values and needs. This, of course, is simply specu-
lation, since we do not know whether occupational practice
will actually satisfy these values. Our point is to indicate
that the potentiality for matching particular individual values and needs with occupations which may satisfy them is
strong. Even if perfect matching does not occur, however, the

principle of psychological distance, discussed in Chapter II, would suggest that the individual can at least find an occupation which will satisfy one of his psychologically contiguous values.

If students hold certain attitudes which appear to be conducive to ultimate occupational adjustment, there are also certain problems for the individual and society which our data suggest may occur. We pointed out earlier that there appear to be certain advantages for social productivity and individual satisfaction involved in the desire to use one's abilities and to be creative in one's work. The problem here is that in an occupational structure which is becoming increasingly bureaucratized a higher premium may be placed on following the rules and showing consistency and predictability in work than in exercising one's creative, spontaneous talents. A reliance upon self-expression and initiative may have the effect of shaking the balance and disturbing the orderliness of the entire structure. In this case, the occupational value of creativity and self-expression may lead to maladjustment in work. It is true, of course, that if any group in the society is likely to have the opportunity to do creative work, it is probably these college students, for they are the people who tend to become professionals, independent businessmen, or higher-level managers. Nevertheless, the problem is there, and it stands as a possible source of conflict.

It is also important to note that there are various factors which, at first glance, appear to promote occupational adjustment, but may under certain circumstances have the opposite effect. Take, for example, the fact that there is a wide range of values which may be satisfied in work and that there are many occupations from which to choose. This state of affairs may actually induce some degree of dissatisfaction in the individual, not because he cannot find a satisfactory occupation but because he is forced to reject various attractive alternatives. Too many alternatives may produce as much dissatisfaction as too few. Indeed, it is possible that in societies in which the individual's occupation is fixed at birth, people may be satisfied with their occupations because it has never occurred to them to consider any other.

These observations underscore the importance of conducting careful empirical studies of the relationship between the individual's initial attitudes and values toward his work and his ultimate occupational performance. Among investigators who are interested in the utilization of human resources in society, there appears to be a bifurcation between those who

TABLE 2.   Faith in People and the Belief that "College Students' would cheat on an examination if they were sure of not being caught"

"I think most coll-edge students would cheat on an exam..."	Faith in People					
	High 1	2	3	4	5	Low 6
Agree	12	24	26	41	50	63
Disagree	76	64	61	50	41	33
Undecided	12	12	13	9	9	4
N	(233)	(437)	(371)	(261)	(174)	(76)

TABLE 3.   Faith in People and the Belief that "These days a person doesn't really know whom he can count on"

"These days a person doesn't really know whom he can count on"	Faith in People					
	High 1	2	3	4	5	Low 6
Agree	7	11	13	28	40	66
Disagree	88	78	78	63	45	29
Undecided	6	11	9	8	15	5
N	(230)	(433)	(368)	(261)	(174)	(76)

TABLE 4.   Faith in People and the Belief that "Generally speaking, Negroes are lazy and ignorant"

"..Negroes are lazy and ignorant"	Faith in People					
	High 1	2	3	4	5	Low 6
Agree and undecided*	7	12	17	19	26	26
Disagree	93	88	83	81	74	74
N	(233)	(441)	(373)	(261)	(177)	(76)

* Since so few people failed to disagree with the statement, we have combined the *agree* and *undecided* groups.

TABLE 5.   Faith in People and the Belief that "Although some Jews are honest, in general Jews are dishonest in their business dealings"

"...Jews are dishonest in business dealings"	Faith in People					
	High 1	2	3	4	5	Low 6
Agree and undecided*	6	10	13	18	26	23
Disagree	94	90	87	82	74	77
N	(232)	(441)	(373)	(261)	(175)	(76)

  * Since so few people failed to disagree with the statement, we have combined the *agree* and *undecided* groups.

TABLE 6.   Faith in People and the Belief that "There's little use writing to public officials because often they aren't interested in the problems of the average man"

"Little use writing to public officials"	Faith in People					
	High 1	2	3	4	5	Low 6
Agree	12	16	26	27	36	45
Disagree	68	64	54	53	47	40
Undecided	20	18	19	20	17	16
N	(236)	(445)	(376)	(262)	(176)	(76)

TABLE 7.   Faith in People and the Belief that "The general public is not qualified to vote on today's complex issues"

"General public not qualified"	Faith in People					
	High 1	2	3	4	5	Low 6
Agree	32	46	44	55	55	68
Disagree	53	44	44	40	38	29
Undecided	10	10	11	6	7	3
N	(232)	(430)	(366)	(260)	(174)	(76)

TABLE 8.   Faith in People and the Belief in the Relative Effectiveness of the United Nations and the Atom Bomb as Deterrents against War

"Which do you, personally, count on as the more effective deterrent against war?"	Faith in People					
	High 1	2	3	4	5	Low 6
The atom bomb	33	44	49	59	55	74
The United Nations	63	51	48	41	40	22
No answer	4	5	3	5	5	4
N	(236)	(445)	(376)	(262)	(176)	(76)

TABLE 9.   Faith in People and the Belief that "The most we can hope to accomplish is the partial elimination of war"

"Most we can accomplish is partial elimination of war"	Faith in People					
	High 1	2	3	4	5	Low 6
Agree	32	39	43	50	52	59
Disagree	21	43	44	40	33	36
Undecided	17	18	13	10	15	5
N	(236)	(445)	(376)	(262)	(176)	(76)

TABLE 10.   Self-Confidence and Tendency to Assume Leadership in a Group (Men)

"How often do you find yourself taking a position of leadership in a group you are with?"	Self-Confidence				
	Low 1	2	3	4	High 5
Often or sometimes	54	59	80	83	87
Occasionally, rarely, or never	46	41	20	17	13
N	(91)	(332)	(453)	(202)	(70)

TABLE 11.   Self-Confidence and Willingness to Give Orders to Others (Men)

"How much does it bother you to have to give orders to other people?"	Self-Confidence				
	Low 1	2	3	4	High 5
Bothers me very much	9	9	5	5	1
Bothers me a little	51	52	43	40	29
Doesn't bother me at all	40	39	52	55	70
N	(90)	(332)	(449)	(200)	(69)

TABLE 12. Belief that "You can't afford to be squeamish"
and "It's who you know more than what you know that counts"

"It's who you know that counts"	"Can't afford to be squeamish about means"		
	Agree	Undecided	Disagree
Agree	47	22	19
Undecided	16	32	15
Disagree	37	36	66
N	(210)	(125)	(786)

TABLE 13. Belief that "In order to get ahead...you have to
be able to make people do what you want" and "You can't afford to be squeamish about the means you use"

"You can't afford to be squeamish about the means you use"	"You have to be able to make people do what you want"		
	Agree	Undecided	Disagree
Agree	22	12	16
Undecided	10	19	9
Disagree	68	68	75
N	(611)	(161)	(361)

TABLE 14. Belief that "In order to get ahead...you have to
be able to make people do what you want" and "It's who you
know more than what you know that counts these days"

"It's who you know more than what you know that counts..."	"You have to be able to make people do what you want"		
	Agree	Undecided	Disagree
Agree	28	17	23
Undecided	16	22	16
Disagree	56	60	61
N	(606)	(160)	(358)

TABLE 15.   Items Included in the "Big Business Minded" Scale

Philosophies of Government:
  1. The best government is the one which governs least.
  2. Democracy depends fundamentally on the existence of
      free business enterprise.

Business and Labor:
  3. If there is no ceiling on business profits, there is a
      better chance to develop better products at lower
      cost.

Right of Private Employers to Hire and Fire:
  4. The individual employer should sacrifice this privilege
      for the social welfare.

*Right to a Free College Education for People Who Meet Require-
      ments:*
  5. Taxes are high enough now.

Right to Free Medical Care:
  6. Would lead to higher taxes and our taxes are high
      enough.

Privileges of Ideal Government:
  7. Unrestricted right of any employer to hire and fire his
      own employees.

TABLE 16.   Items Included in the "Socialism-Planning" Scale

Philosophies of Government:
  1. The best government is the one which governs least.
  2. Government planning almost inevitably results in the
      loss of essential liberties and freedom.
  3. The "welfare state" tends to destroy individual initia-
      tive.
  4. Individual liberties and justice under law are not pos-
      sible in socialist countries.

Right to Free Medical Care:
  5. People might learn to rely on the government for every-
      thing.

A FRAMEWORK FOR THE ANALYSIS OF THE RELATIONSHIP BETWEEN ENDS AND MEANS

In Chapter VIII, we considered the relationship between the goal of monetary success and the adoption of socially disapproved means to achieve this goal. The springboard for this analysis was the paradigm of modes of individual adaptation presented by Merton in "Social Structure and Anomie."[1] Starting with this basic schema, we broadened the scope of our inquiry to examine differences in the range of "morally neutral" and "socially advocated" means adopted by people valuing money, and inquired whether the acceptance of institutionally illegitimate means necessarily involved the rejection of approved means.

It is useful to make explicit the implicit formal scheme which is the basis for the elaboration in Chapter VIII of Merton's means-ends schema. What we have attempted to do is to elaborate one section of Merton's paradigm. Merton's "conformist" and "innovator" types are based on the following combination of elements.

	Modes of Adaptation	Culture Goals	Institution-alized Means
I.	Conformity	+	+
II.	Innovation	+	-

By observing that there are a number of the + and - institutionalized means, that the use of one does not necessarily exclude the use of the other, and that morally tolerated means may also be utilized, we find that, *among those who accept the culture goal of monetary success*, there are not two, but eight, possible modes of adaptation.

Culture Goal
(Accepted)
Institutionalized Means

	(Advocated)	(Tolerated)	(Disapproved)
1.	X	X	X
2.	X	X	--
3.	X	--	X
4.	X	--	--
5.	--	X	X
6.	--	X	--
7.	--	--	X
8.	--	--	--

X indicates use of means; — indicates non-use of means

Such formal elaboration widens our perception of the range of potential modes of adaptation and serves as a more adequate framework for the analysis of the empirical data. Type 2 would probably correspond to Merton's "conformist" type, and Type 5 to his "innovator." Other types—e. *g*., 3, 6, and 8—are unlikely to exist. This framework could be contracted by eliminating the "tolerated" group, since it is empirically unlikely that any people would *completely* eschew socially tolerated means of success. On the other hand, it could be elaborated enormously by differentiating the many different specific types of advocated means, tolerated means, and disapproved means employed by different people. While it is true that such a framework would be very cumbersome, it would nevertheless have the virtue of taking into account all possible combinations of means utilized by those accepting the goal of monetary success. The methodological point is that, while it may not be possible actually to analyze all these possibilities, the formal framework forces us to make a conscious decision regarding those we would consider in our analysis and those we would disregard.

QUESTIONNAIRE

Three bodies of data were employed in the analysis of occupational choices and values. The first was based on a
questionnaire administered to 2,758 Cornell students in 1950,
the second on a questionnaire administered to 1,571 Cornell
students in 1952, and the third on a questionnaire administered to a nationwide sample of 4,585 college students (including Cornell) in 1952. The two 1952 studies were identical, except in two respects: first, some additional questions were included in the Cornell questionnaire which did
not appear in the nationwide questionnaire; and second, ref-
erences to Cornell were omitted from the nationwide studies,
and phrases such as "college students" or "your university"
were substituted. All three studies dealt not only with occupational choices and values but also with educational values, religious values, political and economic values, family
values, and other subjects. In order to indicate the range
of areas covered, certain questions dealing with these top-
ics, as well as all the questions referring to occupational
choices and values, are included in the questionnaire which
follows.

Questions appearing only in the 1950 Cornell study are
marked *A*, those only in the 1952 Cornell study are marked *B*,
those in all three studies are marked *C*, those in both the
1950 and 1952 Cornell studies are marked *D*, and those in the
1952 Cornell study and the 1952 nationwide study are marked
E. The sequence of questions in the appended questionnaire
has been changed from the original studies.

What is your college?

X	2-year course
O	4-year course
1	Architecture
2	Arts and Sciences
3	Engineering
4	Home Economics
5	Hotel
6	I. & L. R.
7	Other:

Your year in college?

Y	1st
X	2nd
O	3rd
1	4th
2	5th
3	Other:

Age at last birthday?

5	Under 18
6	18 or 19
7	20 or 21
8	22 to 25
9	Over 25	C

Sex: 8   Male; 9   Female

What is the size of your home town?

Y	Less than 2500
X	2500 - 5000
O	5000 - 15,000
1	15,000 - 50,000
2	50,000 - 200,000
3	Over 200,000

What is your cumulative average?

In which of these four groups do you consider your family to be?

1	Upper class
2	Middle class
3	Working class
4	Lower class	E

C How would you say you feel most of the time—in good spirits or in low spirits?

1	Very good spirits
2	Fairly good spirits
3	Neither good nor bad
4	Fairly low spirits
5	Very low spirits	E

C Compared with other students you know at Cornell, are you more or less likely than most to be asked your opinions and advice?

Y	More likely to be asked
X	Less likely to be asked
O	Don't know	D

C How often do you find yourself taking a position of leadership in a group you are with?

1	Often
2	Sometimes
3	Occasionally
4	Rarely
5	Never	E

C Would you say that you are the sort of person who finds it easier or harder to make friends than most people?

C 1	Easier
2	About the same
3	Harder	D

How important is it to you, for you to be well liked by different kinds of people?

1   Very important
2   Fairly important
3   Fairly unimportant
4   Very unimportant   E

How much does it bother you to have to give orders to other people?

1   It bothers me very much
2   It bothers me a little
3   It doesn't bother me B
     at all

How much does it bother you to be given orders by someone else?

1   It bothers me very much
2   It bothers me a little
3   It doesn't bother me E
     at all

How important is it for you to have your plans for the future rather clearly known to you in advance?

1   Very important
2   Fairly important
3   Not very important
4   Not at all important E

Are you the sort of person who lets things worry you or don't you let things worry you?

1   Let things worry me
     very much
2   Let things worry me
     quite a bit
3   Let things worry me
     somewhat
4   Don't let things
     worry me   B

Some people say that most people can be trusted. Others say you can't be too careful in your dealings with people. How do you feel about it?

O   Most people can be
     trusted   E
X   You can't be too careful

Would you say that most people are more inclined to help others, or more inclined to look out for themselves?

O   To help others
X   To look out for them-
     selves   E

How important to you, personally, is it to get ahead in life?

1   Very important
2   Fairly important
3   Not very important
4   Very unimportant   E

If you had your choice, which of the following would you *most* like to be? (Check only one)

1   Independent
2   Successful
3   Well liked   B

When you are in a group do you prefer to make the decisions yourself, or do you prefer to have others make the decisions?

1   Usually prefer to make
     decisions myself
2   Usually prefer to have
     others make decisions
3   Not sure which I prefer

                                B

Do you think you cut classes more or less often than most students you know?

1   More often
2   About as often
3   Less often   D

What 3 things or activities in your life do you expect to give you the most satisfaction? (*Please write 1 in space preceding the most important; 2 in space preceding next most important; 3 in space preceding third most important*)

RANK *three:*

Career or occupation
Family relationships
Leisure-time recreational activities
Religious beliefs or activities
Participation as citizen in affairs of your community
Participation in activities directed toward national or international betterment   C

What business or profession would you *most like* to go into?

                                         C

What business or profession do you realistically think you are *most apt* to go into?

Y   Same as above
        Other:
            Specify

                                         C

About how much money do you expect to earn per year about 10 years after you're through with school (assuming present buying power of dollar continues)?

$ C
9   Don't expect to be working

What did your father do for a living at the time you were born?

                                         A

What does he now do for a living?

                                         A

About how much was your father's income last year as far as you know? (If your father is not the chief breadwinner in the family, indicate income of main earner.)

X   Less than $3000
Y $3000 - $5000
0       $5000 - $7500
1       $7500 - $10,000
2       $10,000 - $20,000
3       $20,000 - $30,000
4   Over $30,000   C

How do you expect your own future standard of living (economic income) to compare with that of the family in which you were brought up?

6   Higher standard
7   About the same
8   Lower standard   A

What two qualities on this list do you think really get a young person ahead the fastest today? (Check two)

Y   Hard work
X   Pleasant personality
0   Brains
1   Knowing right people
2   Good luck
3   Being good politician   C

If you could have your own choice in the matter, what kind
of FIRM or OUTFIT would you like best to work in after you
finish your schooling? (Check the one you would like best)

1   Own business or own farm
2   Own professional office
3   Educational institution
4   Social agency
5   Other nonprofit organization
6   Government bureau or agency
7   Military service
8   Family business or enterprise
9   Private firm, organization, factory

        Other: (Specify)   C

Now, aside from your own preference in the matter, what kind
of firm or outfit do you think you are realistically most
likely to end up working in?

1   Own business or own farm
2   Own professional office
3   Educational institution
4   Social agency
5   Other nonprofit organization
6   Government bureau or agency
7   Family business or enterprise
8   Private firm, organization, factory

        Other: (Specify)

Y   Probably will not work   D

When they reported their requirements for an IDEAL JOB or
PROFESSION, students said it would have to satisfy certain
requirements. Some of these requirements are listed below.
As you read the list, consider to what extent a job or career
would have to satisfy each of these requirements before you
could consider it IDEAL.

Indicate your opinion by writing:

  H (high) next to the requirements you consider highly im-
    portant
  M (medium) next to the requirements you consider of medium
    importance
  L (low) next to the requirements you consider of little or
    no important, irrelevant, or even distasteful to you

The ideal job for me would have to...   (Indicate H, M, L)

A. "Provide an opportunity to use my special abilities
    or aptitudes. "

B. "Provide me with a chance to earn a good deal of
    money. "

C. "Permit me to be creative and original. "

D. "Give me social status and prestige. "

E. "Give me an opportunity to work with people rather
    than things. "

F. "Enable me to look forward to a stable, secure
    future. "

G. "Leave me relatively free of supervision by others. "

H. "Give me a chance to exercise leadership. "

I. "Provide me with adventure. "

J. "Give me an opportunity to be helpful to others. "

Now GO BACK and look at the requirements you rated "high. "
Rank them in the order of importance to you by writing next
to each H:

1 for the most important
2 for the next in importance

and so on, for all the H's on your list. Do *not* rank the M's
and L's.   C

Do you think the job or career you have selected as your life
work will satisfy most of the requirements you marked H, some
of them, or only a few?

1   Will satisfy most of them
2   Will satisfy some of them
3   Will satisfy few of them
4   Will satisfy none of them   E

When you think of the qualities that will get a young person
ahead in the field you have chosen, which of the following
ones would you say are *essential?* (Check as many as you feel
are *essential*)

Y	An ability to express yourself	6	Ability to convince and persuade other people
X	A special talent or aptitude	7	Devotion to the work
		8	High degree of intelligence
O	Luck	9	Knowledge of special techniques
1	Leadership ability		
2	Ability to get people to like you	Y	Lots of hard work & effort
		X	Knowing influential people
3	Understanding of other people	O	Having good social poise (know-how)
4	Good grounding in basic theory	1	Having capital or access to it
5	Practical knowledge of facts in your field	2	Organizing and administrative ability A

a. When you think of the qualities that will get a young person ahead in the field you have chosen, which *two* of the following would you say are most important?

b. Now check those qualities which you realistically think you, *yourself*, possess to a satisfactory degree. (Check as many as apply to you)

	Check the *two* that are most important	Check all you think you have
Practical knowledge of theory and facts in your field	1 _____	1 _____
Ability to convince and persuade other people	2 _____	2 _____
Lots of hard work and effort	3 _____	3 _____
Organizing and administrative ability	4 _____	4 _____
Personality	5 _____	5 _____
High degree of intelligence or other special aptitude	6 _____	6 _____ B

Do you agree or disagree with the following statements about getting ahead? Circle the A if you agree, the D if you disagree, and the ? if you are not sure.

"In order to get ahead these days...   Agree Disagree ?

30. "you can't afford to be squeamish about the means you use."   A   D   ?

32. "you have to be able to make people do what you want."   A   D   ?

34. "you really have to love your work."   A   D   ?

B

Which do you, personally, count on as the more effective deterrent against war, the atom bomb or the United Nations?

O   The atom bomb
X   The United Nations   E

HERE IS AN IMAGINARY SITUATION:

Mr. Winthrop is an old family friend whom you know and
like. Business has been pretty bad for some time now, and
he is worried.

He manufactures a plastic gadget which could easily compete
with a rival steel product, except for one thing:

A federal tax on Mr. Winthrop's product raises its final
price, so that it sells for almost the same amount as the
steel product.

Just last week, Mr. Winthrop learned that his steel-product
competitors, in an effort to make sure that this tax is retained, had hired a Washington lobbyist, notorious for
shady tactics in persuading, bribing, and even blackmailing
Congressmen to get them to support his bills.

At a meeting of the Board of Directors of his plant, Mr.
Winthrop is offered the following solutions. Which *single
one* would you counsel him to follow? (Check one below)

Check *one*:
1. Go along as they have been
2. Start a high-powered publicity campaign to secure
    public support against the tax
3. Hire a lobbyist, but be sure he is reputable
4. Hire a lobbyist, but let him use the same tactics
    as the steel lobbyist

WHAT DO YOU THINK MOST BUSINESSMEN IN MR. WINTHROP'S POSITION
WOULD DO? (Check one)
1. Go along as they have been
2. Start a high-powered publicity campaign to secure
    public support against the tax
3. Hire a lobbyist, but be sure he is reputable
4. Hire a lobbyist, but let him use the same tactics
    as the steel lobbyist

In your opinion, is lobbying legal or illegal? (Check one)
9   Legal
O   Illegal
X   I don't know   A

College students have different ideas about the MAIN PURPOSES
OF COLLEGE EDUCATION. Some of their ideas are listed below.
As you read this list, consider what educational goals you
think the IDEAL college or university OUGHT TO EMPHASIZE.
Indicate your opinion by writing:

H (high) next to the goals you consider highly important in
   a university
M (medium) next to the goals you consider of medium importance
L (low) next to the goals you consider of little importance,
   irrelevant, or even distasteful to you (Indicate H, M, L)

A. "Provide vocational training; develop skills and
   techniques directly applicable to your career."

B. "Develop your ability to get along with different
   kinds of people."

C. "Provide a basic general education and appreciation
   of ideas."

D. "Develop your knowledge and interest in community and
   world problems."

E. "Help develop your moral capacities, ethical standards
   and values."

F. "Prepare you for a happy marriage and family life."

Now GO BACK and rank the ones you rated H by writing next to
each H: C

1 for the most important
2 for the second most important

and so on for all the H's on your list. Do *not* rank the M's
and L's.

How do you feel about your   Have you changed your major
major or probable major?   field of study since you en-
                                  tered college?
1   I don't know what it is
    like yet   1   No, and I am not consider-
2   I haven't chosen one yet   ing changing
3   Very interested in it   2   No, but I am considering
4   Fairly interested in it   changing to:
5   Not interested in it
6   Not sure how I feel   3   Yes, I have changed my
                          B   major to:
                                                            E

Students' ideas about the qualities they are seeking in an
IDEAL MATE vary considerably. Here are some, but not all,
of the qualities they said they are seeking, *ideally*. As you
read the list of qualities, consider what qualities you,
yourself, are seeking in an IDEAL MATE. Indicate your ideas
by writing:

H (high) next to those traits you consider highly important
for your mate to have
M (medium) next to the qualities you consider moderately
important
L (low) next to those qualities you consider of little importance or even distasteful   (Indicate H, M, L)

A. "Possesses social know-how. "
B. "Sexually stimulating. "
C. "Has money at time of marriage. "
D. "Interested in having a family. "
E. "Competent in his (her) vocation or profession. "
F. "Very much in love with you. "
G. "Someone with whom you are very much in love. "
H. "No previous sex experience. "
I. "Well groomed and neat. "   A

Now GO BACK and rank the ones you rated H by writing next to
each H:

1 for the most important trait
2 for the trait next in importance

and so on for all the H's on your list. Do *not* rank the M's
and L's.

Right of Private Employers to Hire and Fire:
A   ?   D   The individual employer should sacrifice this
privilege for the social welfare.   A

Business and Labor:
A   ?   D   If there is no ceiling on business profits, there
is a better chance to develop better products at
lower cost.   A

Right to a Free College Education:
A   ?   D   Taxes are high enough now.   A

Right to Free Medical Care:

A ? D   People might learn to rely on the government for everything.
A ? D   Would lead to higher taxes and our taxes are high enough.   A

Philosophies of Government:

A ? D   The best government is the one which governs least.
A ? D   Democracy depends fundamentally on the existence of free business enterprise.
A ? D   Government planning almost inevitably results in the loss of essential liberties and freedom.
A ? D   Individual liberty and justice under law are not possible in socialist countries.
A ? D   The "welfare state" tends to destroy individual initiative.   C

A ? D   The general public is not really qualified to vote on today's complex issues.

A ? D   Although some Jews are honest, in general Jews are dishonest in their business dealings.

A ? D   Generally speaking, Negroes are lazy and ignorant.
                                                                                 C

Do you agree or disagree with these statements about human nature?

A ? D   If you don't watch yourself, people will take advantage of you.
A ? D   No one is going to care much what happens to you, when you get right down to it.
A ? D   Human nature is fundamentally cooperative.   E

Do you agree or disagree with these criticisms of the way things are today?

A ? D   Nowadays a person has to live pretty much for to-day and let tomorrow take care of itself.   E
A ? D   These days a person doesn't really know whom he can count on.

A   ?   D   It's who you know more than what you know that
              counts these days.   E

A   ?   D   There's little use writing to public officials
              because often they aren't really interested in
              the problems of the average man.   E

A   ?   D   I get upset if someone criticizes me, no matter
              who it is.   B

A   ?   D   I usually don't have enough confidence in myself.
                                                                    E

A   ?   D   I think most college students would cheat on an
              examination if they were sure of not being caught.
                                                                    E

CHAPTER I

1. "Soviet Science: Unfathomed Threat," *Carnegie Corporation of New York, Quarterly Report*, Vol. III, No. 1, Jan., 1955, p. 4. These data are based on the work of Alex Korol of the Center for International Studies of Massachusetts Institute of Technology. It is reported that "the Soviet Union may soon be turning out more than twice as many scientists and engineers as the United States... According to members of the project's staff, the best available evidence suggests that the quality of Russian technical education is anything but poor...high-quality scientific education seems to be taking place."

2. *The New York Times*, Dec. 20, 1954, p. 19, quotes the biennial report of the Fund for the Advancement of Education, a unit of the Ford Foundation, as describing the national deficiencies in facilities and teachers as "appalling." The biennial report states: "While elementary and high school enrollments are going up, the number of people preparing to teach is going down. The annual output of elementary and high school teachers has dropped 26 percent since 1950 while enrollments in elementary and high schools have risen 24 percent and 10 percent respectively."

3. Federal Security Agency, *Dictionary of Occupational Titles*, (Washington, D. C.: U. S. Gov't Printing Office, 1949). Cited in Eli Ginzberg, Sol W. Ginsburg, Sidney Axelrad, and John L. Herma, *Occupational Choice* (New York: Columbia University Press, 1951), p. 3.

4. National Opinion Research Center, "Jobs and Occupations: A Popular Evaluation," in R. Bendix and S. M. Lipset, *Class, Status and Power* (Glencoe, Ill.: The Free Press, 1953), p. 417.

5. Clyde Kluckhohn, "Values and Value-Orientations in the Theory of Action," in *Toward a General Theory of Action*, T. Parsons and E. A. Shils, eds. (Cambridge: Harvard University Press, 1952), p. 395.

6. Robin M. Williams, Jr., *American Society* (New York: A. A. Knopf, 1951), p. 375.

CHAPTER II

1. C. Wright Mills, *White Collar* (New York: Oxford University Press, 1951), pp. 215-220.

2. *Ibid.*, pp. 230-233.

3. Leo Gurko, *Heroes, Highbrows and the Popular Mind* (New York: Bobbs-Merrill, 1953), pp. 69-70.

4. See Appendix A, Table 1, for matrix of coefficients of association.

5. Paul F. Lazarsfeld and Patricia L. Kendall, *Radio Listening in America* (New York: Prentice-Hall, 1948), pp. 32-33; and Hans Zeisel, *Say It with Figures* (New York: Harpers, 1947), pp. 27-29.

6. Babette Kass, "Overlapping Magazine Reading," in *Communications Research, 1948-1949*, P. F. Lazarsfeld and F. Stanton, eds. (New York: Harpers, 1949), pp. 130-151.

7. The measure of the adequacy of the matrix in Table 2 is the degree to which the figures in any line or column grow progressively less positive (or more negative) as they proceed away from the diagonal dashes. Theoretically, "the values on the base line (the diagonal adjacent to the dashes) would be high, and these values would progressively decrease, proceeding toward the point of the pyramid (extreme upper right- and lower left-hand corner)," *ibid.*, p. 140, at which point the most negative relationship would appear.

    An examination of the matrix in Table 2 shows that it approximates this model, although it is by no means perfect. If we assume that a failure to decrease positively, or increase negatively, as one moves away from the diagonal dashes, represents an error, then we find that there are seven errors out of a possible 42, an error of 17 percent. Kass (*ibid.*, pp. 140 and 142) has noted that the pattern can be highlighted "by taking the averages of the diagonals parallel to the dashes. Were the correlation perfect, the diagonal immediately adjacent to the dashes would yield the highest average, the next diagonal the next highest, and so on to the most distant diagonal whose average would be the lowest." Going from the outermost to the innermost diagonals, we obtain the following averages:

    Diagonal farthest from dashes   -.386
                                     -.188
                                     -.020
                                     -.099
                                     +.040
    Diagonal adjacent to dashes   +.389

    It will be noted that as one proceeds away from the diagonal adjacent to the dashes, the degree of positive relationship decreases (or negative relationship increases) with the exception of the third diagonal (average = -.099). The reason for this unexpectedly high average is that it includes the very strong negative relationship existing between a desire to be "helpful to others" and to "earn a good deal of money" (Q = -.336).

8. The weighted average was arrived at in the following way: A weight of 4 was assigned to people selecting a particular value alternative as first choice, 3 for second choice, 2 for all other high choices, 1 for medium choice, and 0 for low choice. Since each value complex consisted of two value alternatives, it was possible for each individual to choose one value alternative as first choice and another as second choice; this produced a weighted average for each value complex ranging from 0 to 7. It may be felt that a negative value would have been more appropriate for the low choices, but since our interest was solely in establishing a base for comparing occupations, this weighting procedure appeared adequate for descriptive purposes. It must be recognized, of course, that the procedure obscures bi-modality, but we found no cases of occupations in which large proportions selected the same value alternative as very high and very low, with a small proportion between.

9. We have omitted those answering "don't know" on either wave.

10. Unpublished manuscript.

CHAPTER III

1. Descriptions of the Guttman technique may be found in the following publications: Louis Guttman, "A Basis for Scaling Qualitative Data," *Am. Soc. Rev.*, Vol. 9, 1944, pp. 139-150; Louis Guttman, "The Cornell Technique for Scale and Intensity Analysis," *Educ. and Psych. Meas.*, Vol. 7, 1947, pp. 247-280; Louis Guttman, *in* Samuel A. Stouffer, *et al.*, *Measurement and Prediction* (Princeton: Princeton University Press, 1950), Ch. 3 and 6; Edward A. Suchman and Louis Guttman, "A Solution to the Problem of Question 'Bias'," *Pub. Opin. Quarterly*, Vol. 11, 1947, pp. 445-455; Edward A. Suchman, "The Logic of Scale Construction," *Educ. and Psych. Meas.*, Vol. 10, 1950, pp. 79-93.

2. *A* stands for agree, *D* for disagree, and *?* for undecided.

3. Actually, the selection of these five items represented the end product of several prior operations. In the 1950

study, a number of social and political questions which might be interpreted as reflecting faith in people were found to scale, using the Guttman criteria. The Guttman Scale provides a good measure of unidimensionality, but the single dimension is defined by the manifest content of the items used. The problem now became a theoretical rather than a methodological one. Granted that the questions were tapping the same attitudinal dimension, was this dimension really "faith in people"? Guttman scaling could rank people along both the manifest and the latent content of the dimension, but it could not define the dimension theoretically. While we felt that the implicit dimension of these items actually was "faith in people," it seemed extremely difficult, in view of the fact that the manifest content of the items dealt with social and political questions, to defend this interpretation.

Consequently, when the 1952 study was planned, a series of questions was inserted directly tapping the manifest content of the dimension "faith in people." In order to guard against the danger of subjective interpretation, however, the following steps were taken: (1) A total of 36 items in both questionnaires, which might in any fashion be related directly or indirectly to the dimension "faith in people," were culled. (2) Five faculty members of the Department of Sociology and Anthropology at Cornell University were requested to sort these items into piles reflecting aspects of interpersonal relations. This method differed from the Thurstone item analysis, of course, in the sense that the experts were to determine the dimensions themselves rather than ranking the items with reference to a specified dimension (as well as differing in other ways). (3) Three or more of five judges agreed that nine of the 36 items dealt with "faith in people." (4) An attempt was made to scale these nine items using the Guttman method, and five of these items showed sufficient freedom from error to indicate that they were actually on the same dimension. The coefficient of reproducibility for these five items was .92.

This scale satisfies the Guttman criteria for adequacy in two ways: (1) It is above the minimum standard set for reproducibility; (2) the manifest content of the data refers to the same dimension. The various filtering processes cited above insured objectivity, and the reader will be able to judge for himself whether "faith in people" is the common variable.

The scale fails to satisfy the Guttman criteria for adequacy in the following ways: (1) One of the items, "Human nature is fundamentally cooperative," lacks the 80-20 positive-negative marginal standard established by Guttman as a criterion for inclusion in the scale. This criterion is included to insure against spuriously high reproducibility. Since the other four items together have a reproducibility above .90, however, it seemed to do no harm to include this item, thus increasing our discrimination of groups along the continuum. (2) The scale contains only five items, whereas Guttman claims that at least ten items are essential to serve as an adequate sample of the universe of content. This represents a limitation to the degree of reliability of the scale. However, it is relevant to point out a technical problem in this connection. In constructing a Guttman Scale, we select a sample from a pool of items which deal with the same manifest content. When our items consist of questions, it is impossible to know the total population of items which might be part of the dimension; hence our items cannot be completely random, but must be based on those questions of which we happen to be able to think. Obviously, then, the larger the number of items utilized and the more completely they cover the range of the dimension in question, the more reliable will be the scale. However, as Leon Festinger has noted in "The Treatment of Qualitative Data by 'Scale Analysis'", *Psych. Bull.*, Vol. 44, 1947, pp. 149-161, there are serious practical difficulties of questionnaire and interview administration in asking about the same general attitudinal area in ten or more different ways. Hence, in this case, our scale-type score on "faith in people" represents a compromise between the theoretical requirements of a reliable Guttman Scale and the practical limitations imposed by the questionnaire situation.

4. It is reasonable to challenge the description of "personnel work" as a "helpful" occupation. It may be argued that personnel is one of the manipulative professions—fitting people to do jobs. But the personnel worker (1) does not try to sell himself, (2) does not manipulate people for his own ends, (3) is alerted to the positive qualities of others, and (4) is concerned with helping them make occupational adjustments. His orientation is quite different, then, from that of the sales-promotion person, who seeks to persuade others for his own ends.

5. See Appendix A, Tables 2 through 9.

6. Robert S. and Helen M. Lynd, *Middletown in Transition* (New York: Harcourt, Brace and Co., 1937), p. 404.

7. *Ibid.*, p. 406.

8. Robert K. Merton, "Social Structure and Anomie," in *Social Theory and Social Structure* (Glencoe, Ill.: The Free Press, 1949), p. 132.

9. Robin M. Williams, Jr., *American Society* (New York: A. A. Knopf, 1951), p. 390.

10. John F. Cuber and Robert A. Harper, *Problems of American Society: Values in Conflict* (New York: Holt, 1948), pp. 356-368.

11. *And Keep Your Powder Dry* (New York: Morrow, 1943), passim.

12. Gunnar Myrdal *et al.*, *An American Dilemma* (New York: Harpers, 1944), p. 210.

13. Erich Fromm, *Escape from Freedom* (New York: Rinehart, 1941), Ch. VII, part 2, passim.

14. Karen Horney, *The Neurotic Personality of Our Time* (New York: Norton, 1937), Ch. 15.

15. Karen Horney, *Our Inner Conflicts* (New York: Norton, 1945), Ch. 4.

16. *Op. cit.*, p. 393.

CHAPTER IV

1. *Op. cit.*, p. 201.

2. *Op. cit.*, Ch. V.

3. For a description of this type, see David Riesman, with Nathan Glazer and Reuel Denney, *The Lonely Crowd* (New Haven: Yale University Press, 1950).

4. *Op. cit.*, pp. 21-22.

5. *A* stands for agree, *D* for disagree, and *?* for undecided.

6. Since the majority of women did not expect to be working ten years after graduation, we will consider only the male respondents at this point.

7. Even in college, the self-confident person is much more likely than the anxious one to assume leadership in his groups and is much more willing to give orders to other people. See Appendix A, Tables 10 and 11.

8. Theodore M. Newcomb, *Social Psychology* (New York: Dryden, 1950), Ch. 11.

9. *Our Inner Conflicts*, op. cit., Ch. 3-5.

10. *Ibid.*

11. The types described in this section are intended to approximate the types which Horney has described on the basis of her clinical investigations.

CHAPTER V

1. To our respondents, this factor is of overwhelming importance. Given a list of nine characteristics describing an "ideal mate," 90 percent stipulated that this person be "very much in love with you," and an equal proportion emphasized that it must be "someone with whom you are very much in love."

2. See, for example, Robert K. Merton and Alice S. Kitt, "Contributions to the Theory of Reference Group Behavior," *Continuities in Social Research: Studies in the Scope and Method of "The American Soldier,"* R. K. Merton and P. F. Lazarsfeld, eds. (Glencoe, Ill.: The Free Press, 1950), pp. 40-105.

3. *E. g.*, Richard Centers, "Occupational Mobility of Urban Occupational Strata," *American Sociological Review*, Vol. 13, 1948.

4. Kingsley Davis, *Human Society* (New York: Macmillan, 1949), p. 111.

CHAPTER VI

1. Many of the students who had participated in the 1950 Cornell study had graduated by 1952; hence, it was not possible to follow them up. However, there were 944 people who participated in both the 1950 and 1952 studies, and these respondents constituted the membership of our panel.

2. Cornell University has no School of Social Work and offers only a few undergraduate courses in this field.

3. Eli Ginzberg, Sol W. Ginsburg, Sidney Axelrad, and John L. Herma, "The Problem of Occupational Choice," *American Journal of Orthopsychiatry*, Vol. 20, 1950, pp. 195-196.

4. The basic framework for this form of panel analysis has been developed by Paul F. Lazarsfeld in Robert K. Merton and Paul F. Lazarsfeld, "Friendship as Social Process; A Substantive and Methodological Analysis," in *Freedom and*

Control in Modern Society, edited by M. Berger, T. Abel, and C. H. Page (New York: Van Nostrand, 1954), pp. 18-66.

5. It must be remembered, of course, that one reason for this fairly close relationship is that social selection has narrowed down the aspirations of these primarily middle-class college students to a limited range. For example, as we noted in Chapter I, their social environments are such that they give virtually no consideration to thousands of manual occupations.

CHAPTER VII

1. *E. g.*, Talcott Parsons, "Propaganda and Social Control," *Psychiatry*, Vol. 5, 1942, pp. 551-572, and the forthcoming work by Robert K. Merton and William J. Goode on the sociology of the medical profession.

2. Ginzberg *et al*, "The Problem of Occupational Choice," *op. cit.*, p. 187.

3. This result, of course, is partly an artifact of the small number of cases. It does not mean that no women will enter business, but rather that the *proportion* decreases—there probably are fewer new female entrants into business than abandoners.

4. See Lazarsfeld's discussion of this subject in Robert K. Merton and Paul F. Lazarsfeld, *op. cit.*, pp. 47-49.

5. *Ibid.*

CHAPTER VIII

1. Robin M. Williams, Jr., *op. cit.*, p. 390.

2. This is essentially a male value; in this chapter, therefore, we will deal with the men in our sample.

3. *Op. cit.*

4. *Ibid.*, p. 129.

5. *Op. cit.*, p. 436.

6. Robert K. Merton, *op. cit.*, pp. 134-135.

7. This result is not attributable to the low faith in people of the money-oriented person. Both the desire for money and faith in people exercise an influence independent of each other with regard to all items dealing with means of getting ahead. The cumulative impact of these two variables is particularly strong. For example, 93 percent of the most misanthropic, money-oriented men agreed (or were undecided) that "You can't be too squeam-

ish about the means you use," compared with only nine
percent of the non-money-oriented men with the highest
faith in people.

8. The only exception is found among those who are not concerned with getting ahead. So few of these people were
interested in making money that we cannot judge the influence of the desire for money at this level.

9. This relationship exists irrespective of faith in people.
In fact, when we consider the cumulative impact of money-
orientation and faith in people on the belief that "It's
who you know that counts," 93 percent of the misanthropic,
money-oriented people agreed with the statement, compared
with 27 percent of the non-money-oriented respondents with
high faith in people.

10. The only exception to this statement appears among those
who consider success irrelevant; here the results are inconsistent.

11. This statement refers to the official success ideology
which stresses achievement rather than ascription of
status. Actually, stratification literature reveals that
the appropriate style of life may contribute more to the
individual's social status than the acquisition of money
through effort. See, for example, W. Lloyd Warner and
Paul S. Lunt, *The Social Life of a Modern Community* (New
Haven: Yale University Press, 1941), pp. 98-99.

12. Herbert Goldhamer and Edward A. Shils, "Types of Power
and Status," *American Journal of Sociology*, Vol. 45, 1939,
p. 171.

13. This relationship holds irrespective of degree of faith
in people.

14. See Appendix A, Tables 12, 13, and 14.

15. A suggested framework for the analysis of the relationship
between means and ends appears in Appendix B.

CHAPTER IX

1. Valuable discussions of the new middle class can be found
in Lewis Corey, *The Crisis of the Middle Class* (New York:
Covici-Friede, 1935), and C. Wright Mills, *op. cit.*

2. This figure accords closely with the corresponding figure
of 78 percent for the nationwide sample noted in Chapter
VII.

3. The items constituting these scales will be found in
Appendix A, Tables 15 and 16.

4. Richard Centers, *op. cit.*

CHAPTER X

1. Ernest Havemann and Patricia Salter West, *They Went to College* (New York: Harcourt, Brace & Co., 1952), Ch. 3.

APPENDIX B

1. *Op. cit.*, p. 133.